Judith Spelman is a writer and journalist who lives in Lincolnshire. She started in journalism as a researcher/assistant to the literary editor of the *Montreal Star* in Canada, going on to spend several years immersed in the publishing industry in England. Over the years she has worked on local and national newspapers and trade and consumer magazines. For the past fifteen years she has earned a living as a full-time freelance writer and editor. *Lincolnshire Bedside Book* is her fourth book.

LINCOLNSHIRE BEDSIDE BOOK

A Collection of Prose and Poetry

SELECTED AND INTRODUCED BY
JUDITH SPELMAN

THE DOVECOTE PRESS

This book is dedicated to my son, Guy Wyles, and
to John and Tom Wyles and their families, whose
roots go deeply into south Lincolnshire.

First published in 2003 by The Dovecote Press Ltd
Stanbridge, Wimborne, Dorset BH21 4JD

ISBN 1 904349 23 4

© Introductions, Judith Spelman 2003

Typeset in Monotype Sabon
Printed and bound by The Baskerville Press Ltd.
Salisbury, Wiltshire

A CIP catalogue record for this book is available
from the British Library

1 3 5 7 9 8 6 4 2

CONTENTS

INTRODUCTION

Lincolnshire is much maligned as a county. It is big, originally stretching eighty miles from north to south and fifty miles from west to east. It is not conventionally beautiful, but it has a wildness that captures the imagination and a charm that lingers and satisfies. Do not take anything at face value in Lincolnshire: dig deeply into its past, query its present and enjoy your discoveries.

Some people dismiss Lincolnshire as flat and boring. What nonsense! Flat in places, true, but this allows us to witness the vast Fenland skies, or as Charles Kingsley says, 'the arch of Heaven', so typical of this part of eastern England. Early mornings sees the night sky fade to grey with clouds tinged with cream and apricot. Dusk adds more colours – greens, indigos, yellow, orange and reds – until the blackness falls.

The long straight roads across the Wolds, the Marshes, the woods, the Fens and the streams have all inspired writers through the centuries. Many were born in the county, some have visited – and stayed – and others have just passed through.

There is a richness of fine market towns, a coastline that has that has survived many batterings from the North Sea and a farming heritage that once produced the finest longwool sheep and shorthorn cattle

It was difficult to decide what to include and what to leave out as there is so much that has been written about the county. This book had to be a personal choice of extracts; things that I have found interesting, funny, fascinating or just plain informative about Lincolnshire. I have done a minimal amount of editing to make some of the older extracts easier to read but I think you will find in many the little idiosyncrasies of the writer creeping through. I hope you agree that is a bonus but I cannot vouch for the accuracy of other people's work.

As this is a bedside book readers probably will dip into it before they sleep, or, if they are fitful sleepers like me, they could read extracts in the middle of the night. I have tried to make sure there is nothing included that might encourage nightmares!

Selecting the extracts for this book has been sheer indulgence. I have enjoyed every minute of my researches and I hope that now you will enjoy reading some of my discoveries.

When she heard I was compiling the *Lincolnshire Bedside Book*, the poet Doris Corti wrote a poem celebrating the county's character:

Lincolnshire

Today the wind moves clouds across the sun
and shadows criss-cross
the fields of Lincolnshire, Marsh and Wolds,
rivers and sky caught in a lattice work of variable light.

The roads that Romans built stretch to the horizon
and towns and little villages, farms and fens
bring recognition that the past and present merge;

the same old rituals persevere,
fields are ready for the plough and on the coast
waves are turning with the tide;

while here, on my way home, ancient inns and abbeys
and church spires are silhouetted
against a backdrop that is sky.

JUDITH SPELMAN, *October* 2003

I · THE FENS, WOLDS AND MARSHES

The Fens, the Wolds and the Marshes give Lincolnshire its character. Many writers are lyrical when they describe in detail the differences of these distinct parts of the county. I love the way Charles Dickens thinks of the county as "moist", and the way Tennyson writes of the "calm and deep peace" of the Wolds. M. W. Barley, in his introduction to Lincolnshire and the Fens *explains the nature of the county.*

When Dickens wanted a dreary setting for Lady Dedlock's country place in *Bleak House,* he chose Lincolnshire, and he planted it in a dripping landscape populated only by rabbits, crows, and sodden deer. Scott in *Peveril of the Peak* had Roger Wildrake style himself "of Squattlesea Mere in the moist county of Lincoln". The truth is that Lincolnshire and the Fens are the driest part of England. One misconception of nineteenth-century novelists has died, but another untruth has taken its place. It is commonly thought that Lincolnshire is flat. The Lincolnshire man's rebuttal takes a double form: first, the county is not flat, and second, if it is flat, that flatness is the essence of its character and particular beauty.

Mr. Harry Batsford's advice when we first discussed this project was that I should not be too much on the defensive. I have not been consciously more so than Cowper was when he wrote:

> Scenes must be beautiful which, daily viewed
> Please daily, and whose wealth survives
> Long knowledge and the scrutiny of years.

Cowper, Constable, and de Wint found a beauty in the English lowlands which is still there, little altered, for anyone to see who wishes, though it requires a more lively eye than do the highlands. Lincolnshire belongs especially to Peter de Wint, who found a lifelong friend in William Hilton of Lincoln, married his sister Harriet Hilton, and came back time after time to fix for ever the qualities of the Lincolnshire landscape in those wide, low watercolours. George Crabbe, another lowland poet, who belongs as much to that part of the Vale of Belvoir where Kesteven, Nottinghamshire, and Leicestershire meet as he does to the Suffolk coast, wrote of the Fens:

> All are appropriate, bog, marsh, and fen,
> Are only poor to undiscerning men.

I claim no more discernment than anyone else, but I have enjoyed making the effort to convey in words something of the evolution of this man-made countryside. I have encountered the difficulty that anyone must feel in writing about his own county: one knows at once too much and too little – too much to be able to select and too little to do justice to one's sentiments.

M. W. *Barley*, Lincolnshire and the Fens, *(1952), Preface. p. v.*

Wet Weather at Chesney Wold

While Esther sleeps, while Esther wakes, it is still wet weather down at the place in Lincolnshire. The rain is ever falling, drip, drip, drip, by day and night, upon the broad flagged terrace-pavement, The Ghost's Walk. The weather is so very bad, down in Lincolnshire, that the liveliest imagination can scarcely apprehend its ever being fine again. Not that there is any superabundant life of imagination on the spot, for Sir Leicester is not here (and, truly, even if he were here, would not do much for it in that particular), but is in Paris, with my lady; and solitude, with dusky wings, sits brooding upon Chesney Wold.

There may be some motions of fancy among the lower animals at Chesney Wold. The horses in the stables - the long stables in a barren, red-brick courtyard, where there is a great bell in a turret, and a clock with a large face, which the pigeons who live near it, and who love to perch upon its shoulders, seem to be always consulting - they may contemplate some mental pictures of fine weather, on occasions, and may be better artists at them than the grooms. The old roan, so famous for cross-country work, turning his large eyeball to the grated window near his rack, may remember the fresh leaves that glisten there at other times, and the scents that stream in, and may have a fine run with the hounds, while the human helper, clearing out the next stall, never stirs beyond his pitchfork and birch-broom. The grey, whose place is opposite the door, and who, with an impatient rattle of his halter, pricks his ears and turns his head so wistfully when it is opened, and to whom the opener says, "Woa grey, then, steady! Noabody wants you today!" may know it quite well as the man. The whole seemingly monotonous and uncompanionable half-dozen, stabled together, may pass the long wet hours, when the door is shut, in livelier communication than is held in the servants' hall, or at the Dedlock Arms; - or may even beguile the time by improving (perhaps corrupting) the pony in the loose box in the corner.

So the mastiff, dozing in his kennel in the courtyard, with his large head in his paws, may think of the hot sunshine, when the shadows of the stable buildings tire his patience out by changing, and leave him, at one time of day, no broader refuge than the shadow of his own house, where he sits on end, panting and growling short, and very much wanting something to worry, besides himself and his chain. So, now, half-waking and all-winking, he may recall the house full of company, the coach-houses full of vehicles, the stables full of horses, and the out-buildings full of attendants upon horses, until he is undecided about the present, and comes forth to see how it is. Then, with that impatient shake of himself, he may growl, in the spirit, "Rain, rain, rain! Nothing but rain, - and no family here!" as he goes in again, and lies down with a gloomy yawn.

So with the dogs in the kennel-buildings across the park, who have their restless fits, and whose doleful voices, when the wind has been very obstinate, have even made it known in the house itself: upstairs, downstairs, and in my Lady's chamber. They may hunt the whole country-side, while the rain-drops are pattering round their inactivity. So the rabbits with their self-betraying tails, frisking in and out of holes at rots of trees, may be lively with ideas of the breezy days when their ears are blown about, or of those seasons of interest when there are sweet young plants to gnaw. The turkey in the poultry-yard, always troubled with a class-grievance (probably Christmas), may be reminiscent of that summer morning wrongfully taken from him, when he got into the lane among felled trees, where there was a barn and barley. The discontented goose, who stoops to pass under the old gateway, twenty feet high, may gabble out, if we only knew it, a waddling preference for weather when the gateway casts its shadow on the ground.

Be this as it may, there is not much fancy otherwise stirring at Chesney Wold. If there be a little at any odd moment, it goes, like a little noise in that old, echoing place, a long way, and usually leads off to ghosts and mystery.

Charles Dickens, Bleak House, *(from Chapter VII) pp. 85-87.*

The Second Largest County

Lincolnshire is the second largest county in England and the least appreciated. The long North Sea coast-line and the indentations of the Humber and the Wash make it an isolated kingdom of its own, another country almost, whose associations are with the sea and with Denmark and Holland rather than with England and the English midlands.

The landscape is of two strongly contrasted kinds - one long and level with two-thirds of every eyeful sky. Into this, medieval stone towers and spires, trees and hedges, the pylons, poles, wires and tractors of our own day are easily assimilated. Wide and splendid cloudscapes and a great expanse of stars at night will remain here however much the surface landscape changes and the power lines multiply. The other sort of scenery is hilly, the rolling country of the Wolds, which seem very high by contrast but never rise more than 550 ft. and are like the Downs, with beech plantations on their slopes and villages in their hollows and at their feet. The rain has made deep ravines which are not often seen unless you are on horseback or on foot, for the roads tend to follow contours.

There is a second distinction to be made in the two sorts of level Lincolnshire; that is to say between Marsh and Fen. The Marsh is the low land of narrow dykes, meres and pools which stretches along the sea coast between the wash and the Humber. The east wind constantly blows over it from the North Sea, the water in the dykes is brackish with salt that has percolated through the sand. These are areas of rich pasture land, stiff grass and wild fowl. The Fen is not salt, nor is it near the sea except in small patches. Most of it is drained silt-land, ditched and dried out to produce rich cornland and fields for bulbs and flowers.

Two very different ridges extend down the county from the Humber, widening out as they go southwards. The easterly one is chalk - the Wolds - and widens and then fades into the Fens by Spilsby and Horncastle. For some miles south of the Humber the crest of the Wolds is windswept, and Danish raids from the sea come to mind again. The string of villages nestles under the western edge of the ridge, sheltering from wind and the Dane: Caistor and Normanby dominate the Ancholme Valley westwards. To the east is the wooded country of the Earl of Yarborough's estate, and from these parts you may look back northward to the industrial Humber bank, to the great fish port of Grimsby, or down towards the spire of Louth or across the marshes to the caravans and holiday camps of Cleethorpes, Mablethorpe, Sutton and Skegness. The southern end of the Wolds has vantage points, too, from which you may look over the rich, drained Fen to Boston Stump and beyond. West Keal and Asgarby are good for this purpose.

The narrow western ridge is called Lincoln Heath, or "Cliff", and is here a straight and tenuous limestone backbone. Its beginnings are in Yorkshire across the Humber, and southwards it crosses England by way of the Cotswolds and into Somerset. There are two gaps in this backbone – at Appleby and at Lincoln; but otherwise it runs its course, never much more than a mile wide, for forty miles before it broadens into the Shires, the land of stone houses amid parks and trees and shady villages in prosperous country towards Grantham and Stamford.

Jack Yates & Henry Thorold, Lincolnshire, A Shell Guide, *(1965) pp. 9-12.*

Lincolnshire Wolds and Lincolnshire Sea

Lincolnshire Wolds and Lincolnshire Sea
Calm is the morn without a sound,
    Calm as to suit a calmer grief,
    And only thro' the faded leaf
The chestnut pattering to the ground;

Calm and deep peace on this high wold,
    And on these dews that drench the furze,
    And all the silvery gossamers
That twinkle into green and gold;
Calm and still light on this great plain
    That sweeps with all its autumn bowers,
    And crowded farms and lessening towers,
To mingle with the bounding main;

Calm and deep peace in this wide air,
    These leaves that redden to the fall,
    And in my heart, if calm at all,
If any calm, a calm despair;

Calm on the seas, and silver sleep,
    And waves that sway themselves in rest,
    And dead calm in the noble breast
Which heaves but with the heaving deep.
Alfred, Lord Tennyson.

Moulding the Wolds

It is easy to be passionate about the Lincolnshire landscape but to write about it evocatively, so that cynics will wonder and look again, is a gift.

South of Caistor the western scarp is not a steep one; the clays mask it and the first sign of Wold as one goes east is clumps of beeches, which are most at home on chalk mixed with some clay. The Wolds rise to no great height – 548 feet above Normanby-le-Wold – but high enough to give those enormous views, to which neither pen nor camera can do justice, with Lincoln and Boston Stump, the Humber, and the Wash as their farthest landmark. One eighteenth-century traveller disliked such views because they were "like an embankment into eternity"; they are more to our taste than to his.

The Ice Age moulded the Wold landscape into a varied pattern; north of Caistor is a low, smooth ridge with enough clay mixed with the chalk to make good farm land and suitable ground for Lord Yarborough's miles of plantations. South of Louth the chalk is in places eroded down to the sandstone that underlies it, giving a more broken type of scenery and a quite different flora. Although the ice rode over even the crest of the central Wolds, and left behind Scandinavian erratics such as the blue stone which gave its name to the prehistoric ridgeway, the Blue Heath Road, it left fine swelling uplands above the clay-filled green valleys in which the villages lie. In summer the expanse of ripening corn "clothes the Wold and meets the sky"; and those who know only the chalk downs of the south, where there is more permanent grass, ought to see this county in the spring, when there is the subtlest interplay of the greens of young corn and the brown soil over the chalk on the great ranging slopes. Man is scarcely noticed in such a landscape, for the population is thin, like the soil, thinner than anywhere else in the county. The villages are perfectly sited by their streams; some are charming, but many are nondescript, and some are almost squalid, for there is no background of wealth to give the buildings any substance or quality. Many of the small churches had to be rebuilt in the nineteenth century; by the time the Methodist chapels were built Victoria's reign was half over and the chances of a good building gone.

M.W. Barley, Lincolnshire and the Fens, (1952), p.20 - 21.

Lincolnshire: from the Wolds to the Fens

Alken: Know ye the witch's dell?
Scathlock: No more than I do know the walks of Hell
Alken: Within a gloomy gimble she doth dwell
        Down in a pit, o'ergrown with brakes and briars,
        Close by the ruins of a shaken abbey
        Torn, with an earthquake, down unto the ground,

'Mongst graves, and grotts, near an old charnel house,
Where you shall find her sitting in her form,
     As fearful, and melancholic, as that
     She is about; with caterpillar's kells,
     And knotty cobwebs, rounded in with spells;
     Thence she steals forth to relief, in the fogs,
     And rotten mists, upon the fens, and bogs,
     Down to the drowned lands of Lincolnshire;
     To make ewes cast their lambs.

Ben Jonson, The Sad Shepherd, *11, vii, pp. 13-27.*

The Marsh

*There is a tract of marshland that lies between the Wolds and the
North Sea. Nowadays it is about ten miles wide but once, before the
sea gradually eroded the coast line and broke through the sand dunes,
it was much wider. It was here that saltmaking developed as an
important Lincolnshire industry.*

The marsh has been wrested from the sea in a struggle that goes back
to the Romans, and even at the beginning of the last century the
ditches between Wainfleet and Spalding were filled with salt water
and twenty-thousand acres drowned when the Bank gave way at
Boston. The "Old Sea Bank" marks one stage of the grim advance.
Over the new bank are "the flats", a wilderness of samphire beds and
tiny rivulets of salt water, a world whose silence was once only broken
by the cry of stint and curlew and the sound of a Wash fisherman's
cart. The treachery of the currents is shown by an entry in St Mary's
register [Wainfleet] to the effect that in 1806 two sailors were
"drowned in an unfortunate attempt to reach the shore, their vessel
having grounded on the flats". Not so long ago, "flight nets" could be
seen along the shore on dark, moonless nights, especially on
"November darks". It is interesting to note that in 1512 seagulls,
plovers and redshanks fetched three-halfpence apiece, lapwings, knots
and dotterels a penny, and that in the middle of the 17th century
Lincolnshire was known as "the aviary of England".

The Revd. J. E. Swaby, MA, Wainfleet, (1930), pp. 4-5.

A View of the Stump

Edward Storey is a Fen man, born and bred, and his understanding and love of the Fens is evident from the eloquent way he writes about them.

Lincolnshire mist, like south Lincolnshire soil, is born of the sea, or so it appears to be. It is different from the mist of the Cambridgeshire fens which rises from the earth, smells of the earth and is often as heavy as the earth. The mist of Lincolnshire is more phantom-like, transparent and (if you will forgive the unavoidable pun) mysterious. It has a strange quality of light about it, an opaqueness which does not erase everything from view but rather enhances it with subtle nuances. The sky becomes no more than a window which has been breathed on. Beyond the misty glass can still be seen the outlines of the familiar, but the familiar is changed. I am speaking now of early autumn mists rather than winter fogs – for I know of no county which can produce worse fogs than Lincolnshire.

A recent journey reminded me of this distinction, of this unusual effect which Lincolnshire mist has upon me, as well as upon the land. It smells of the sea and swirls like the sea. It even carries echoes of the sea and has the threat of the sea. The encounter of which I write happened one day as we were making our way home from the Wolds. My wife was driving, so I could concentrate on the exciting transformation going on around me. We were, as usual, taking the roads 'less travelled by' and were in no particular hurry. The day had been warm but sultry, with the occasional thunderstorm, and there was certainly a mist out at sea when we ventured towards the coast. That mist now crept inland, and the fields were wrapped in a grey muslin which made them look unreal and insubstantial. The harvest was over, and, as there had been less stubble-burning this year, each cornfield had the appearance of a deserted beach at sunset. The straw shone like fine sand. The dark horizon was a distant sea.

Immediately the familiar landscape took on an excitement – or, rather, I became excited about the familiar. Trees drifted in and out of my vision like a ballet of ghosts. Church spires emerged and then melted away more quickly than ice before a fire. The mist did not hover knee-deep as it does so often in the Cambridgeshire fens; it enveloped everything from the sky down.

On the long, straight road from Revesby down to Frithville, I had the feeling that I had embarked on a journey into the unknown, a journey which could at any moment reveal some wonder or miracle.

I did not have long to wait. As we turned towards Gipsey Bridge, then crossed the River Witham towards Brothertoft, the mists thinned sufficiently for Boston Stump to appear like a faded sepia print on a Victorian sky. I have never seen the stump (a most inappropriate nickname on this occasion) look so tall, so elegant and so ethereal. It was etched delicately but briefly on my afternoon, yet I know the memory of it will survive the mists of many years.

I cannot explain why some moments
equal a lifetime, why some seconds
carve fissures quicker than waterfalls.
but it's always happening. The mind
dwells for a journey upon one thought
that suddenly is shattered by a glimpse
of someone chopping wood, a woman
just unlocking her front door, and then . . .

And this time was the moment of that elongated tower, made more of the stuff of visions than earthly stone that was meant to last forever.
Edward Storey, Spirit of the Fens, *(1985), pp. 159 – 160.*

The Lost Tides

The poet, Doris Corti, lives in the Fens. This is how she imagined them in her poem.

Earth quickens under dyke roads,
draws sustenance from the salt of secrets.

Each moon keeps the secret, tugs at the tides
and the channelled run by hidden shores,
forgotten sea, and marshland dune.

White, belligerent clouds dominate black fields
and space; against the skyline, like projected film,
a boy and his dog leap on a dyke road
playing age-old rituals of run, and chase.

A curious beauty here, in light undiminished
by shadows of trees and hills. Only the gulls
know the secret ways, where air
stings salt over ploughed drills.
They follow lost tides, skimming the air
With wings unfurled, sky-gliding,

while the boy embraces the day
and the turning moon still rides.

Doris Corti

2 · LINCOLN, TOWNS & PLACES

Lincolnshire is generally considered an agricultural county but there are some important industrial towns as well as the city of Lincoln, the fine market towns, villages and hamlets. This is merely a selection of writings by authors who express definite views; whether you agree with them is something for you to decide.

The Eighteenth Century

There appears to have been some foundation for Bishop Fuller's criticism of Lincolnshire that no county possessed better churches or worse houses. Travellers were not impressed favourably by the towns. Ruin and desolation appeared everywhere in the city of Lincoln in 1725, and the very cathedral itself was in imminent danger of becoming a rubbish heap. Daniel Defoe found Barton 'a straggling mean town noted for nothing but an ill-favoured dangerous ferry.' Grimsby was a good town, but Defoe considered the anchorage dangerous and many ships had been sunk there in the Great Storm of 1703. Boston was large, populous and well built, and Grantham was similarly described. Market Deeping, however, was ill-built and dirty, both of which adjectives were applied in 1772 to Donington and Swineshead. To Thoresby, the Yorkshire antiquary, Stamford was a scurvy dear town, while to Byng it was large but ill-built, without shade around it or manufactory within it. Byng, however, was in search of a 'stomatic' medicine at the time, which may account for his jaundiced opinion of one of the most delightful towns in the country. *Charles Brears,* Lincolnshire in the Eighteenth and Nineteenth Centuries, *(1940), p.103.*

A Noble Structure

Daniel Defoe journeyed throughout the country at the beginning of the eighteenth century and wrote down his conclusions on the state of economic and social affairs in a graphic and colourful manner. Although he admired Lincoln Cathedral, he was less impressed by the division between the two halves of the city.

Lincoln is an antient [sic], ragged, decay'd, and still decaying city; it is so full of the ruins of monasteries and religious houses, that, in short, the very barns, stables, outhouses, and, as they shew'd me, some of the very hog-styes, were built church-fashion; that is to say, with stone walls and arch'd windows and doors. There are 13 churches, but the meanest to look on that are anywhere to be seen. The cathedral indeed and the ruins of the old castle are venerable pieces of antiquity.

The situation of the city is very particular; one part is on the flat and in a bottom, so that the Wittham [sic], a little river that runs through the town, flows sometimes into the street, the other part lies upon the top of a high hill, where the cathedral stands, and the very steepest part of the ascent of the hill is the best part of the city for trade and business.

Nothing is more troublesome than the communication of the upper and lower town, the street is so steep and so strait [sic], the coaches and horses are oblig'd to fetch a compas another way, as well on one hand as on the other.

The River Wittham, which as I said runs thro' the city, is arch'd over, so that you see nothing of it as you go thro' the main street; but it makes a large lake on the west side, and has a canal, by which it has a communication with the Trent, by which means the navigation of the Trent is made useful for trade to the city; this canal is called the Foss-dyke.

There are some very good buildings, and a very great deal of very good company, in the upper city, and several families of gentlemen have houses there, besides those of the prebendaries and other clergy belonging to the cathedral.

This cathedral is in itself a very noble structure, and is counted very fine, though I thought it not equal to some that I have already describ'd, particularly not to that at Litchfield. Its situation indeed is infinitely more to advantage, than any cathedral in England, for it is seen far and wide; it stands upon an exceeding high hill, and is seen into five or six counties.

The building in general is very noble, and the church itself is very large; it has a double cross, one in the nave or center on which the great tower stands, and one at the east end of the choir, under which there are several antient monuments; the length of the church is near 500 foot, the breadth 126; so that it is much larger than that at Litchfield; but the spires on the towers at the angles at the west end are mean, small, and low, and not to be nam'd with those at Litchfield. The tower is also very plain, and has only four very ill-proportioned spires, or rather pinnacles, at the four corners small and very mean.

The city was a flourishing place at the time of the Norman Conquest, tho' neither the castle or the great church were built. There were then three and fifty parish churches in it, of which I think only thirteen remain. The chief extent of the city then was from the foot of the hill south, and the from the lake or lough which is call'd Swanpool east. And by the Domesday Book they tell us it must be one of the greatest cities in England, whence perhaps that old English proverbial line: Lincoln was, London is, and York shall be.

Daniel Defoe, A Tour Through England and Wales, *(1724), vol.2, pp. 91-93.*

Stamford 1724

Daniel Defoe came to Stamford from Rutland and the North West. He seemed to like the town although he could not understand the governing system.

From hence we came to Stamford; the town is placed in a kind of angle of the county of Lincoln, just upon the edge of three counties, viz. Lincoln, Northampton and Rutland: this town boasts greatly too of its antiquity, and indeed it has evident marks of its having been a very great place in former days.

History tells us it was burnt by the Danes above 1500 years ago, being then a flourishing city. Tradition tells us, it was once a university, and that the schools were first erected by Bladud, King of the Britains; the same whose figure stands up at the King's Bath in the city of Bath, and who lived 300 years before our Saviour's time. But the famous camps and military ways, which still appear at and near this town, are a more visible testimony of its having been a very ancient town, and that it was considerable in Roman times.

It is at this time a very fair, well-built, considerable and wealthy town, consisting of six parishes, including that of St Martin in Stamford-Baron; that is to say, in that part of the town that stands over the river, which, tho' it is not a part of the town, critically speaking, being not in the liberty, and in another county, yet 'tis all called Stamford, and is rated with it in the taxes and the like.

This town is the property, as it may be called, of the Earles of Excester; for the author of the survey of Stamford, page 15, says, 'William Cecil, Baron Burleigh, and afterwards Earl of Excester, obtain'd the fee farm of Queen Elizabeth for himself, in whose posterity it yet remains.'

The government of this town is not, it seems, as most towns of such note are, by mayor and aldermen, but by an alderman, who is chief magistrate, and twelve comburgesses, and twenty four capital burgesses, which, abating their worships' titles, is, to me, much the same thing as a mayor, aldermen and a common council.

Daniel Defoe, A Tour through England and Wales, *(1724), vol.2, pp.104-105.*

The Cathedral

In the 1980s author and journalist Danny Danziger came to Lincoln to write about the city and was entranced by the Cathedral. He interviewed forty people whose lives revolved around the building to get an insider's view of its character and atmosphere. These are the views, and a little about the work, of three of them; the Clerk of the Works, the Verger and the Precentor.

Dr John Bailey, Clerk of Works.

Because they were generally built of local stone, each cathedral has its own particular characteristics. Lincoln has a colour that is fairly unique, this warm brown, nicotine-colour stone is iron and stone which gives it a curious, rich colour. English churches tend to be low and fat, a slightly dumpy, pregnant sort of look to them, whereas Lincoln is tall and thin and slender, and, of course, its siting on the edge of the escarpment means that it is set in a very dramatic location, particularly coming from the south side, where you see it up on the horizon.

My first sight of it was the view from the road coming in from the east, where you see it with three fingers pointing up, and if you see that in the dusk, it really is a stunning experience. I was visiting Gothic buildings everywhere, I wasn't just coming here. It was an accident in the first instance coming across Lincoln amongst a lot of other cathedrals. But I think Lincoln does have a certain grip on people, that when they experience that shock of seeing it for the first time, and walk around in it, it's a sort of love affair. And once it's hit you, you don't forget it.

If you walk around the Cathedral, you don't need to be an expert to see how the chemical impurities in the atmosphere are attacking the stone. You can see the stone sort of peeling off, as though it is bursting from inside, and that is purely the attack of sulphates - and that is all over the whole Cathedral. The rate of decay and attack by pollutants is such that we are actually running as fast as we can but still going backwards.

There is nothing dramatic happening, like the tower falling down or the West Front falling off; what you've got here is a multiplicity of minor crises. Each one in itself is no big deal, but multiply these by the hundred and you start to get an understanding of the problem. One the stone side we have this perpetual chemical attack on the physical face of the stone. Lead that covers the roofs is a marvellous material, but after sixty years, or something like that, it starts to get fatigue, just like metal fatigue in aircraft; it's expanding and contracting with the heat and the cold and in the end it cracks. That means water gets through and rots the timber underneath, so you've got to strip the lead off to repair the timber, which has been rotted by water or attacked by beetles, then put it all back again.

My predecessors have been sitting here since 1150, looking after this Cathedral in its various shapes and sizes, and there is no reason why it can't go on. There is a feeling that if those people could keep the place going, surely to God you can. I don't think you would do this sort of job if you didn't have some kind of love affair with the building - you don't get people working here for the money. On a summer's evening, at eight o'clock, if you just go into the Cathedral all by yourself, nobody else is there, it's absolutely quiet and there is that almost green evening light coming into it, all the strain and stress just drifts away. It's the most astonishing thing.

Katie Middleton, Verger

We run the place. We're the housekeepers if you like. We open up in the morning and lock up at night. We prepare services, we officiate at services, we make sure it's generally tidy and clean and just keep an eye on things to make sure everything runs smoothly.

First of all in the morning I unlock all the doors and I walk around the cloisters, but I open the cloisters last of all. Then I look up at the big tower from the north side. It's lovely if the sun's shining, but if it's misty you can only see half the tower. But you can see the kestrels and the pigeons and the blackbirds. We had a blackbird's nest in the cloisters and we watched the baby ones grow up.

You've got to be able to work long hours and you've got to be quite strong. If we have to put all the chairs out in the nave, for example, it's an entire day of physically hard work. There are 2,000 chairs. There's a lot of walking involved. You have to wear flat, thick-soled shoes to cope with the stone floors.

I think it's good wearing a cassock because people can spot us from a long way off and see that it's someone official, and it sets us apart. On Sundays and for special services we wear a blue cassock, with a white jabot, which is a sort of neck cloth. Otherwise we wear black gowns and white gloves; very smart, don't you know. We like to think we are the best turned-out cathedral vergers.

The Reverend David Rutter, Precentor

I think no one can fail to be impressed by the Cathedral. For myself, I suppose it is a love relationship because the building seems so feminine: this is Our Lady's Church, and one feels her presence all the time. I see the effect it has upon the worshippers who love it as a building and find it congenial to worship here, not only because it is large and grand and lovely, but because there is an atmosphere about it to which they are sensitive, an atmosphere of prayer and devotion, a stillness, and that, I think , moves people to prayer and worship.

The Cathedral has no parish and the people who come, come because they want to. There are a few who are tenants in our properties, and the parents and families of our singers come because of that link. And there are a few, I expect, who are disgruntled and who have fallen out with their parish priest, but not many. Others come because they are drawn by the beauty of the building, sometimes by the services, sometimes by the preaching, and many by the music.

My favourite part of the Cathedral is the place where the Blessed Sacrament is reserved, the Chapel of St Mary Magdalene, because the Blessed Sacrament is the focus of our devotion and therefore to be there is natural. The Morning Chapel, where I hear confessions, is a place that is very sacred to me.

My least favourite activity is worshipping in the winter-time when we have no heat on. It's pretty cold in the cathedral, pretty cold! The organist will tell you that the condensation on the keys actually freezes.

It's very tiresome, my eyesight is going. It's controlled at the moment and with the help of strong lamps and a reading glass I can manage. I read the office of matins this morning. I have to prepare things very carefully so I don't make mistakes. It takes longer to write letters and there are some letters you can't do through a secretary. Many personal and pastoral letters come to my box, and it's no use having a young girl reading out a letter that begins, 'I am about to leave my husband, what do I do next?'

There is a hackneyed phrase that it's a challenge; but it is. It puts you on your mettle in the sense that you can't let it overcome you.

Danny Danziger, The Cathedral, *(1989), pp. 13-15, 121-122 and 162-163.*

Burghley House

Although Burghley House is just over the county border, it is so closely allied to Stamford that one easily forgets this. The home of the Cecil family for centuries, their fortunes and misfortunes have been chronicled in prose and poetry.

At the end of the seventeenth century Celia Fiennes (1662-1741) took long journeys throughout England, writing and commenting in shrewd detail on what she observed. This extract is taken from her records of travels 'from Amwell by Cambridge and Lincoln to Nottingham' in 1697 when she comes across Burghley House and the town of Stamford.

Stamford town is as fine a built town all of stone as may be seen. It is on the side of a hill which appears very fine in the approach; severall very good churches with high Spires and Towers very ornamentall, its not very large but much finer than Cambridge, and in its view has several good houses; on the right hand of Stamfford is a house of Mr Neals, in a pretty neat parke pailed in. The house not very big but lookes well; on the side of the hill over against Stamfford and on the left hand over against the town stands my Lord of Exeters Burly [Burghley] House eminent for its Curiosity; the Scituation [sic] is the finest I ever saw on the edge of the hill and severall rows of trees and severall acres above it quite to the Road, it stands in a very fine parke which is full of deer and fine rows of trees.

Christopher Morris (ed), The Journeys of Celia Fiennes, 1698, (1947), pp. 67-68.

A Vast Hill

After visiting Burghley House, Celia Fiennes continued north to Stretton, eventually reaching Lincoln.

. . . thence to Colson [Colsterworth] where Lincolnshire comes in, 2 mile, thence towards Lincoln we go on a fine champion country much like Salisbury Plaine, and a large prospect all round at a distance; you see woods and towns, this is the best part of this shire, for most part is fenny; and we went twenty six miles all on such way quite to

Lincoln town, we pass by Grantum (Grantham) which is a good town 16 mile from Lincoln, all built with Stone but lies down in a low bottom, the Church has a very high Steeple. It's seen above a great hill that is by it of a great length, and 'tis a long tyme when you see a great part of the Steeple ere you come to see the Church or town, it lies so in a bottom.

Lincoln opens to view at least 6 miles off. It stands on a very high hill and looks very fine at the entrance, the houses stand compact together the Streetes are but little, but it's a vast hill to ascend into the town where the Minster stands, by that meanes its very perspicious (sic) and eminently in view a great many miles off; the tower that Great Thoms Nest is 250 steps up, 8 persons may well stand up in the hollow of the bell together, its as much as a man can reach to the top of the bell with his hand when he is in the inside, its rarely ever rung but only by ringing the Clapper to each side – which we did – and that sounds all over the town; the houses are but small and not lofty nor the Streetes of any breadth; the Sea has formerly come up to the town and that has been very deep water where now great part of the town is built, so that what was the town formerly is that which stands upon a precipice as it were of a hill, the water is choaked up now and the Sea comes not near in severall miles and what water they have is called Lincoln Dike, you pass over it on a bridge.

Christopher Morris (ed), The Journeys of Celia Fiennes, *1698, (1947), pp. 67-68.*

Botolph's Town

Christopher Marlowe travelled throughout East Anglia and Lincolnshire between the wars, noting the changing characteristics of the counties. From Leverton he reached Boston.

'Botolph's Town' is one of the oldest in Lincolnshire and full of historical associations. In the seventeenth century St Botolph, the guide and patron saint of travellers, founded a monastery here, on the site of which afterwards arose the magnificent parish church. But long before that the Romans built a fort at the entrance to the [river] Witham and established at a short distance to the south of the town.

Three times did fire and flood devastate the settlement, whilst, in the thirteenth century, a certain Robert Chamberlayne and his associates deliberately set fire to the houses and plundered the booths of rich citizens at the great fair. One is glad to read that he paid for his crimes with his life, being 'hanged from the neck until he was dead' in 1288.

The town rose to great prominence in the days of King John, when we read that 'a levy of one-fifteenth on all moveable goods was ordered. This produced in two years no less than seven hundred and eighty pounds fifteen shillings and sixpence' in the coinage of that time.

Then in 1298, Boston paid customs dues to the amount of over thirty-one thousand pounds, this sum being one third more than London paid. In the thirteenth and fourteenth centuries it was not only a great commercial town but a staple port for wool, leather, tin and lead. In the time of Edward the Third it sent no less than seventeen ships and two hundred and sixty men for the invasion of Brittany, and elected deputies to three grand councils at Westminster.

The fifteenth century saw its decline as a port and by the seventeenth century it had become 'decayed and ruined'. But even now [1925] there is a big trade in timber, hemp and tar from the Baltic, fish from the North Sea and exports of agricultural produce. The docks are extensive, with a big market and a stage for fishing boats. In this quarter you see chandlers' shops, old inns with typical seafaring names, rope and tar stores, and other nautical necessities.

Christopher Marlowe, The Fen Country, (1925), pp. 139 - 141.

Grimsby

Another port on the Lincolnshire coast is Grimsby, not always considered a particularly salubrious town. It is rather different these days.

Grimsby appears ninth in a list of thirteen ports from whose merchants 'fifteenths' were levied in 1204. It is recorded that Richard I held a parliament here and that King John visited the town twice, giving it its first charter. These facts show that it was a fairly important port in mediaeval times. During the reign of Edward III, it furnished eleven ships and 171 men for the expedition against France, and they saw service at the siege of Calais. Subsequent decline is said to have been caused by the silting up of the harbour, and by the lack of measures to counteract this. Increase in the size of ships would make such a natural disadvantage more apparent. In 1628, Gervase Holles said: 'Now she (Grimsby) hath but one poor coal ship and scarce mariners in the town to man it.' In the middle of the seventeenth century only the smallest fishing boats could approach the port. Local apathy allowed these conditions to prevail until 1801 when the Old Dock was constructed at a cost of £60,000, and afterwards passed into the hands of the ancestor of the old Manchester, Sheffield and Lincolnshire Railway Company (Great Central).

The Royal Dock was opened in 1854, the Union and Alexandra Docks in 1879 and later, three Fish Docks, three Graving Docks and a Floating Dock; the total water space of the whole system being over 100 acres with a depth from 20 to 26 feet. The accommodation, especially for the fish trade, is inadequate and projects have been discussed to secure the extension of docking facilities. Near the docks are ranges of transit sheds as well as warehouses for grain, bonded goods, raw and manufactured goods and merchandise of every description – such accommodation now, alas, something of a 'white elephant.' Sidings occur in all directions and hydraulic and electric crane equipment is provided whenever transfer is likely. Practically all this plant is the property of British Railways, to the energy of whose ancestor, the 'Company', is due much of Grimsby's rise since the middle of the last century.

John Bygott, Lincolnshire, (1952), p.59.

Grimsby 1764

'The Most Lively Place' John Wesley wrote in his Journal on 3 April 1764. He went on to add that 'here had been a large and swift increase, both of the Society, and hearers, so that the house, though galleries are added, is still too small'. The 'house' referred to, had been completed seven years before. However, this enthusiastic reception had been somewhat different from those he had received on earlier visits to the port. For example, on 17 March 1745 he had written of his congregation that they were 'so stupidly rude and noisy:

encouraged thereto by their forespeaker, a drunken ale-house keeper. I singled him out, and fastened upon him, till he chose to withdraw.' The little preacher's piercing eyes were renowned for quelling the most awkward individuals and rowdy mobs. As you read the accounts of his many visits to the town you have the sensation that he felt for the plight in which Great Grimsby had fallen in the 18th century. He himself summed it up on 19 April 1766 thus: 'It is no bigger than a middling village, containing a small number of half-starved inhabitants, without any trade, either foreign or domestic, but this they have; they love the gospel, hardly six families excepted'.

David Kaye, The Book of Grimsby, (1981), p. 39.

Memories of Simbooth Grange

In 1952, Bryan Forbes, at that time a struggling actor and would-be novelist, and the American writer, William Styron, who had just had his first book published, set off in an ancient Austin Seven on a tour of England which included a nostalgic visit to places he had known as a child.

We set out for Lincolnshire; I thought I would combine business with pleasure and revisit some of my childhood haunts. Both my mother and father had numerous relatives in the fens, the majority of them farmers, and it was there that I had spent most of my early holidays. In particular there was one house called Simbooth Grange, the family home of the Leggatts, distant cousins of my father, that to me retained romantic connotations. It was situated just outside Woodhall Spa and within sight of a small chapel made out of corrugated iron sheets, painted rust red, which on Sunday evenings reverberated and shook as the faithful pitched into rousing Methodist hymns. There was also a Kinema in the Woods, I remember, where the patrons sat in deck chairs, and to a London child the whole area was an alien landscape under wide, Constable skies, where anything could happen.

I remembered Simbooth Grange as being vast, a place where for the first time in my life I had a bedroom to myself, and it had been the inspiration for my, mercifully unpublished, works. Of course it wasn't vast, just a rambling old farmhouse, but to a child sizes appear exaggerated. Rumour had it that there was a secret passage from Simbooth to nearby Crowthorne Abbey that had been used by the priests during the Cromwellian period, and this added to the mystery I weaved in my imagination. The moment one entered the house had an odour all of its own – a mixture of so many things, carbolic soap and rainwater in the damp, stone-flagged kitchen where often laying hens intruded; the slate-cold larder gave off other scents – freshly separated cream stood in an earthenware pot alongside the jar of sugar-water where wasps met their end; bricks of home-made butter were laid out beneath the salted hams and sticky fly papers. There were buckets of brown eggs gathered from the hedgerows, the churn of foamy milk. Stored Bramley apples, big as melons had slept through winter in the darkness and added their musky scent.

It was in Woodhall Spa that I spent the first year of the war – the 'phoney war' as it was termed – a reluctant evacuee compelled for a time to attend the village infant school where, because of my age, they could teach me nothing. I remember solitary bombers droning overhead on their way to drop leaflets into Germany. In those days we went to sleep in feather beds by candlelight and the house groaned during the night as rats scuttled in the eaves. Downstairs one of the rooms had been sealed against a gas attack and the windows sandbagged though, from what I later experienced having returned home just in time for the London Blitz, the crude sanctuary would have offered little protection.

Simbooth Grange and nearby Walcott Dales close to the Norman keep of Tattershall Castle were the first ports of call for Bill and me that trip. I was greeted as a creature from outer space by all the relatives, for they had not seen me since the first year of the war. Then I had been a scrubby schoolboy, but in the intervening years I had not only served in the army, but more impressively I had become an actor, had my name in the papers and been to Hollywood, the only member of the family to achieve a degree of notoriety. Bill and I were received and treated like royalty and stuffed with food. Bill later confessed he had never seen anything like it: breakfasts of home-cured bacon, new-laid eggs, fried bread and potatoes, tea tables laden with whole hams, sausage rolls, a variety of cakes and tarts, for in those days nobody dieted if they could help it and the word cholesterol was unknown. Although farmers lived hard in 1952, they lived well. Many with small acreages still used shire horses for ploughing; sugar beet, one of the staple crops, continued to be cut by hand and only the more affluent could afford electric milking machines. Although the word organic was not yet in general use, most spread animal manure on their land and the eggs were certainly free range, taken warm from the nest and popped straight into the frying pan.

Bryan Forbes, A Divided Life, (1992), pp.231-233.

Horncastle

Just north of Woodhall Spa is Horncastle, a town described by William Cobbett as 'not remarkable for anything of particular value or beauty, a pure agricultural town; well-built and not mean in any way.' Over the years the town has aged well and colourfully. It is hard to believe that this respectable town, twenty miles or so to the north-east of Lincoln, and voted Antiques Town of the Year in 2001, was once rife with prostitution, drunkenness and lowlife. Michael Lloyd explains.

The name of Horncastle was famous throughout the land for its annual horse fair, one of the greatest in England, Europe or the world according to the euphoria of a number of descriptions. For one week in August horse dealers flocked here from all over the country, accompanied by a motley throng of entertainers, card-sharpers, prostitutes and pickpockets. Stories of the fair abound, like that of the unfortunate clergyman who sold his horse for £25 and bought another for £40 only to discover he had bought back his own with a docked tail, clipped mane and the star on its forehead concealed with dye. Some of the dealers used rough methods to drive a bargain, as when a gang of half a dozen cornered an old man to try and force him to sell for £4 a horse which he had paid £14 for; another, according to legend, pursued the vicar into church and settled a price with him at the foot of the pulpit as he came down from delivering his sermon.

The rip-roaring frontier atmosphere of the horse fair must have presented almost insuperable problems for the forces of law and order, and indeed the records show that in the early Victorian period even a small town like Horncastle was a place where drunkenness, prostitution and petty crime abounded. In 1838 the town appointed its first paid police force, of two, later three, constables supplemented when necessary by supernumeraries. The 30s a week needed for a trained officer from London or Hull was considered excessive, and local men were employed for half that wage, one of the first of whom lost his job on being strongly suspected of pandering for one of the towns numerous houses of ill fame. The low-life of a small country town is portrayed vividly in the surviving notebooks of the constables. Innumerable inns and beer-houses, open to all hours, generated drunken brawls: 'tremendous row in Dog Kennel Yard, 2 women fighting, several men of bad character and 5 prostitutes...such a row was never heard in Horncastle before.' Apprentices and labourers were tempted to gamble their money away at skittles, cards – 'Puff and Dart, The Devil among the Tailors, Ringing the Bull' and other such games.

Michael Lloyd, Portrait of Lincolnshire, *(1883), pp. 136 – 138.*

3 · FISHING & FARMING

I came across William Kime's poem 'Lincolnshire' quite by chance. It describes the way in which the seasonal tasks of the farming year continue ceaselessly on, despite great historical events and the passing of the centuries.

> To Lincolnshire the legions led,
> The eagle ensign at their head,
> To lay down laws the Roman way
> And force the people to obey;
> > But still the farmer ploughed his soil,
> > Enriching it through days of toil.
>
> The Saxons and the Vikings came
> To Lincolnshire with sword and flame,
> Fierce pirates in the painted ships,
> Dread heralds of Apocalypse!
> > And yet, the seed each year was sown
> > And crops of rye and barley grown.
>
> When Norman William's cruel hordes
> Split up the land for foreign lords,
> Each free man then a serf became
> And bowed his head in grief and shame;
> > But, in the hazy August heat,
> > The flails were threshing out the wheat.

A thousand years have passed along
> the centuries of right and wrong –
With king and prince, and church and state,
Each trying to predominate;
> Yet, with the good earth biding here,
> Still grows the corn in Lincolnshire.

William Kime,
Suzy Goodall (ed), Eastern England Poets, (1995), p. 122.

The Arrival of the Smacks at Grimsby

There had been occasional landings of sprats in the old dock, but it was the construction of the Great Northern line to London which really made the town into a fishing port. Fishing with the beam trawl, known at Barking and Brixham since about 1800, had led the smacks from the Channel to the North Sea. As the yield of fish from the traditional grounds diminished, grounds further to the north were explored and by 1845 there were forty smacks fishing from Hull. It was at once realised that the position of Grimsby was more favourable if only the fish could be got to London. The town council made this point in petitioning of the East Lincolnshire Railway Company's bill.

Seymour Clark, manager of the Great Northern, persuaded his directors to give a bonus to the firm of James Howard and Company to bring their fleet of thirteen vessels from Manningtree to Grimsby. The first smack to make a landing was probably the *Princess of Württemberg* from Barking, whose skipper later immigrated to Australia and visited friends in Grimsby in 1880. It was in 1850 that she came from barking. The new dock, and the railway to it, were not yet complete and the first box of fish was taken on a cart to the town station, ceremonially escorted by a band, or so he recalled in 1880.

Most of the earliest smacks to come to Grimsby were not equipped for trawling but for catching lobsters and line-fishing for cod. The vessels were fitted with wells from which the catch could be landed alive. When Harrison Mudd came from Brixham as a cabin boy in one of these vessels, the dock tower was only one-third built and they landed in the outfall of the Old Dock and sold the lobsters at Keetley's dry dock. In 1851 up to 7,000 lobsters from the coast of Norway arrived at a single landing and in the course of the year 50,000 were sent to London by rail. By 1853, the *Pearl*, a screw steamer, was bringing lobsters from Norway, discharging 7,000 and several boxes of salmon only eight days after sailing; and the Grimbsy-built smack, *Thomas*, landed 20,000 lobsters after crossing the North Sea in fifty-three hours.

Fishing vessels were built at Grimsby within a year of the commencement of the trade. The Great Grimsby Fishing Co., an enterprise jointly sponsored by the railways, ordered the Thomas from Robert Keetley and in May 1852 she was launched into the Old Dock. In the evening he gave a party for sixty of his men. Seven of the other vessels owned by the Great Grimsby Fishing Co. were built by Keetley, including the *John Ellis*, a schooner with an auxiliary screw, intended for lobster fishing and completed in 1853; and the *George*, a steam screw schooner with a crew of nine for collecting fish from smacks on the Dogger Bank. She appears to be the first steamer used in fleeting, but when she sank two miles off the Humber after a boiler explosion in 1853, she was not replaced.

At first Grimsby was not so much a fishing port as a place from which smacks were trying their luck before moving elsewhere. At the end of each season many of the lobster fishers left Grimsby for the Scottish cod and herring fishery. But very soon the advantages of Grimsby began to attract smacks from other ports. From Hull it was necessary to tow smacks to sea when the wind was unfavourable. Grimsby was on the coast. The advantages were not overwhelming, and for much of the nineteenth century Hull kept pace with Grimsby as a fishing port; but the growth of the industry at Hull did not in any way retard it at Grimsby. There was nothing to tie vessels to one particular port. In 1856 there were hopes, wildly exaggerated that a hundred or more smacks were about to transfer from Barking to Grimsby. In actual fact, fourteen smacks sailed from Grimsby for Iceland and nine of them were from London. Many smacks were expected to leave Hull when the first Grimsby fish dock was opened. It was said that they could land their fish and be back on the fishing grounds in the time which it would have taken them to sail up the Humber to Hull. But in the first year of the fish dock only five transferred from Hull to Grimsby.

Edward Gillett, A History of Grimsby, *(1970), pp. 228-229.*

Rabbit warrening during the eighteenth century

Surely the practice of rabbit warrening shows that farmers were always diversifying on their lands?

The Wold is essentially a region of mixed farming, where sheep rearing, barley growing and turnip culture long predominated, though attention is also given to wheat and other crops, as well as to the raising of live stock. However, not much more than a century ago these branches of the farmers' activity were only carried out in the more favoured spots along the lower slopes of the valleys, where talus furnished an easily worked and fertile soil. The inferior and especially the more sandy areas were largely utilised as rabbit warrens, which supported an industry with peculiar economic significance. It was peculiar because investment of a small capital produced an interest which little else would do, and inferior lands could be used without much outlay for preparation and upkeep. The following is a year's balance sheet quoted by Arthur Young for a farm of 250 acres.

Expenses	£ s. d.	Income	£ s. d
Rent, tithe rates	87 10 0	Carcasses, 2,000	75 0 0
Fencing	15 16 4	(couples at 9d)	
Warrener	40 0 0	Skins, average 1s.	
Extra labour	19 0 0	each	£200 0 0
Nets, traps, charcoal	2 1 6		
Horses (delivery, etc)	7 4 0		
Winter food	10 0 0		
Poison (for foxes			
Powder, shot, etc)	2 0 0		
	183 11 10	Profit: 91 8 2	

Provision of poison for foxes must have caused mixed feelings amongst sportsmen in a hunting county, but the warrener reckoned the fox as much an enemy and an economic liability as does the Australian sheep farmer regard the dingo or wild dog.

Theoretically, the warrens were walled and fenced in, but this was rarely done so efficiently that the rabbits did not escape and do much damage to neighbouring crops. Therefore, they were economically destructive, apart from the fact that the warrens kept large areas out of cultivation – not of much importance before the amelioration of the Wolds, but a weighty consideration when this was done.

In summer the rabbits foraged for themselves but in winter they were fed with turnips, oat straw, clover hay, eked out with ash boughs and gorse, etc. Regular warreners were employed, receiving as high wages as the best paid farm hands (eg, £35 a year, use of a cow, fuel and house, equal in all to about £40). Their duties comprised feeding the rabbits, repairing the walls or fences, clearing away the snow in winter, killing and skinning the rabbits as well as preparing the skins (for which charcoal was used) and they also had to guard against poachers and vermin.

John Bygott, Lincolnshire, *(1952), pp.170-171.*

The Value of Wool

The agriculturalist and writer Arthur Young (1741-1820) was appointed as Secretary to the Board of Agriculture in 1793. He was one of the first people to promote agriculture as a science and spent much time travelling through England and Ireland conducting agricultural surveys and suggesting ways in which farming could be improved. Between 1770 and 1771 he wrote The Farmers Tour *through the East of England.*

When Arthur Young made his tours through the county towards the end of the eighteenth century, he found that much attention had been paid to the improvement of the native Lincolnshire cattle. By a judicious infusion of Dutch, Durham and Yorkshire blood, the red shorthorn breed had been evolved. It is worthy of note that the marked improvement took place from before 1700 to 1750, before the general enclosure of the land. Some writers, however, attribute the origin of the Lincolnshire shorthorns to the cattle which were introduced into the county after the Colling's sale at Ketton in 1810.

The Lincolnshire sheep also were much improved in the seventeenth century. The oolitic and chalk hills in early times had proved suitable grazing grounds, and the county had always exported much wool. In 1631, however, it was stated that the Lincolnshire salt marshes had the largest sheep, 'but their legs and bellies were long and naked, and their staple extremely coarse'. By the beginning of the next century more than one writer testified to the quality of Lincolnshire wool. This was from 10 inches to 18 inches long, and weighed 8 to 16 lbs. per fleece. According to Defoe this county, and Leicestershire, not only produce the largest fleeces in the country, but also the finest wool. It is to the credit of the eighteenth century farmers that they were sufficiently enlightened to improve the native sheep by introducing Leicestershire blood. Arthur Young found that the experiment had been tried with good effect in many parts of the county. He stated that Robert Bakewell had used sheep from Sleaford and Grantham districts in forming the famous Dishley breed of new Leicesters, and others affirmed that Bakewell adopted the practice of letting out rams from Lincolnshire, where it had long been current. However that may be, the new Longwools have been recognised as an established breed of this county since 1750. They were well known since 1785.

Unfortunately for the farmers, the prices obtained for the wool were subject to violent fluctuations. In 1728, owing to rot among the sheep, the maximum price of 30s a tod [28 lbs] was obtained, but prices fell to 11s a tod.in 1782, and there were 250,000 tods unsold in the county. There was a constant agitation to induce the government to allow a restricted export, but, although it was sponsored by Sir Joseph Banks and backed by the landed interest, it was unsuccessful. The Norwich clothiers claimed that the fall in price was one phase of the 'universal stagnation of Trade and Commerce, which was the fatal consequence of a long extended and expensive war.'

Charles Brears, Lincolnshire in the Seventeenth and Eighteenth Centuries, *(1940),*
pp.123-124.

Potato Railways – Rise and Decline

How many people know of the potato railways that criss-crossed the county at the beginning of the last century? Theirs was a short history – less than 50 years – but during that time they provided a valuable link between the potato farmers and their market.

The credit for starting this agricultural transport revolution most probably goes to George Caudwell, a farmer who lived at St Lambert's

Hall, Weston. He was a potato grower experiencing winter haulage problems. He contacted Harry Peacock, one of the co-founders of the well known Lincolnshire agricultural machinery firm of Peacock and Binnington, and asked for a quotation for the supply of a mile length of standard gauge railway on his land. Following discussions over the suitability of such a line, a German firm with great experience in the provision of narrow gauge lines in the West Indian sugar plantations was asked to survey the site, and suggested that narrow gauge would be most suitable. Mr Caudwell was not convinced, but was persuaded when the firm agreed to lay and equip the line for a one year trial. If it was not a success they would make no charge. It was, however, a great success.

These deliberations have not been dated, but it was before 1909. The location of the line is similarly not known definitely, but was most probably part of that centred on Wraggmarsh House, at Weston, from where a branch ran southwards to St Lambert's Hall. The gauge of this line was two feet.

Other lines were built before World War One, which itself proved the use of light railways over very rough, heavy, waterlogged land in France. After this, large quantities of war-surplus track, engines and rolling stock were put on sale. The track was of 60cm gauge, variously quoted as 1ft 11 fi ins, 1ft 11 fl ins, or 2ft gauge. Fenland farmers now seized their opportunity to provide better access to their land, and the heyday of the agricultural narrow gauge line now began.

As far as is known, two weights of rail were used: 20lb per yard on the more intensively worked lines with locomotives, such as Nocton, and 9lb per yard on the lighter, horse worked lines, such as Grange Farm, Holbeach St Marks.

Few lines employed locomotives. The most extensive, those at Nocton, Fleet and Dawsmere, used them for most of their existence, others experimented with them, but the majority used horses. It made sense to do this as there were already horses on the farms, and the railway made their use more efficient. On the heavy land in winter, four horses may be needed to haul one cart loaded with five tons of potatoes out of the fields. Using the railway, on some farms with no gradients, one horse could haul up to six trucks loaded with 10 tons of produce. Another big advantage was that as speeds were so low, certainly on the horse lines, minimal maintenance was required. In their latter years, tractors were used to pull the trucks before replacing the railways completely.

Farmers, large and small, utilised railways. The most prominent potato producer and the greatest user of the railways was the firm of W. Dennis and Sons who owned large estates at Nocton, 8000 acres, Deeping St Nicholas, 2000 acres, and in the Kirton area, 200 acres. Eventually they were to operate over thirty miles of line, 22 miles on their Nocton estate alone.

At the other end of the scale was the line jointly owned by two or more farmers, of whom each would use his own trucks. These were of varying lengths, up to one mile.

Most lines ended adjacent to a hard surfaced public road at which point a dock or shed would be built to facilitate transfer of the produce into carts or lorries for onward trans-shipment. A few also ran to adjacent main railway lines where the goods could be transferred to and from railway wagons. In two cases, the Wraggmarsh House system at Weston and at West Butterwick, there were branches to small wharves, on the Welland at the former, and the Trent at the latter.

Once laid, they tended to become a permanent feature because, although they could be moved around, and some were, it was a major operation. Also, although laid for use in the winter months, once down, most were then used all year round.

In total in Lincolnshire there were 106.5 route miles of track on 34 systems. The high point was the late 1920s when just over 105 miles were in operation at 33 locations. The first closure came in the late 1920s when Dennis's removed 2.25 miles at Littleworth, followed by two there small lines in the 1930s. On the outbreak of World War 11, however, there were still over 98 miles in operation.

The years 1939 to 1945 saw a radical change in British agriculture. The need to produce the maximum amount of home-grown food to reduce imports, together with the loss of skilled land workers to the armed forces, required greater efficiency. This was brought about largely by mechanisation, and the horses that worked on almost every farm in 1939 were largely replaced with tractors by 1945. Many miles of concrete and stone farm roads were constructed to enable vehicles to move easily and the need for the railways fell, almost half of them closing or being reduced during this time. Mechanisation proceeded after the war, and in a few short years the day of the agricultural railway was over.

In 1945, 61 miles remained on 17 systems. By 1950 it had fallen to 38 miles on 10 systems, of which three closed that year reducing the mileage to 31. By 1955, it fell again to 25.5 miles on three systems. Of these three, two closed that year, leaving only that at Nocton to soldier on for a few years longer. Most of it was to be closed in 1960, although one vestige remained in use until 1969.

Today there is very little to be seen of these once busy transport systems. Roadways have replaced many of them. There are no significant earthworks to mark their route. Almost the only remnants are occasional loading docks or goods sheds, fast being removed themselves. Farmers being thrifty people, lengths of rusting rail can be found in farmyards, now being used as supports or fence posts.

Stewart E. Squires, *The Lincolnshire Potato Railways*, (1987), pp. 13-15.

Salt Making

Just to the south of Wainfleet on the west side of the A52 from Boston is a pasture field covered with extraordinary ranks of small, rounded mounds. These are 'saltcotes' or 'salt-hills', examples of which survive throughout the Marsh and the Fens around the Wash. They are visible evidence of an industry which flourished in the area from the Iron Age to the seventeenth century, the evaporation of salt from sea water. The mounds when excavated prove to contain salterns, low, round hearths made of hand bricks (lumps of clay squeezed into shape by hand) covered with the debris of fires and of the earthenware vessels in which the brine was evaporated. A coastline of scrubby country with a clay soil cut by tidal creeks was ideal in providing the raw materials for this industry. In the Iron Age, and more especially in Roman Times, the evidence is even more plentiful from around the Wash than it is from the Marsh. The Roman or pre-Roman Salter's Way, which runs south of Grantham to join the Fosse Way in Leicestershire, was almost certainly a route by which this important commodity was exported to other parts of the country. By the early Middle Ages the main centres of salt-making may have moved northward. The documentary as well as the visible evidence is plentiful: thirteen salterns in the Domesday description of Tetney, for instance. Manorial rents were often paid in salt. In the sixteenth century the Fulstow salters were travelling as far afield as Gainsborough market to sell their goods. The industry, however, seems to have collapsed rather suddenly by the middle of the next century. Holinshed's Chronicle mentions the disaster of the great tide of 1571 when 'all the salt-cotes where the chief and finest salt was made were utterly destroyed to the utter undoing of many a man and great lamentation of old and young'. But one natural disaster could scarcely cause the total collapse of an industry which did not rely on heavy capital investment; no doubt the salterns were repaired. The construction of defensive banks on the seaward side of the saltcotes in the early seventeenth century may have contributed to their decay; or other centres of the industry may have taken over the Lincolnshire salters' markets; or their supply of easily available brushwood for fuel may have run out. Possibly they found that the production of meat was now more profitable than the manufacture of its preservative; at Tetney in 1627 the salt floors were decayed and turned into good pasture for sheep.

Michael Lloyd, Portrait of Lincolnshire, *(1983), pp. 119-120.*

A Major Industry

David N. Robinson goes into more detail as he explains the art and intricacies of the salters.

When Edmund Cowper, salter of Marshchapel, died in 1559 the story of over 2000 years of the making of salt on the Lincolnshire seashore was already drawing to a close. During that time it developed into a major industry, making Lincolnshire one of the country's leading producers. It started towards the end of the Bronze Age when the land began to rise slightly relative to sea level, generating freshwater marsh intersected by tidal creeks. The biggest spread of the industry was during the succeeding Iron Age. The workers in the prehistoric saltmaking industry occupied sites above high spring tide level in scrub country alongside streams flowing off the hills into a series of long tidal creeks through saltmarshes, mudflats and sandbanks which extended into the sheltered tidal lagoon.

Sea water was scooped from the creeks at high tide, or from side channels which had been blocked off to allow the silt to settle and some natural evaporation to take place. It was then poured into shallow U-shaped pottery troughs about two feet long and nine inches across, quite light in weight and porous (the pottery contained chopped grass and chaff with grains of oats and ryegrass). Also scooped from the mud on the banks of the creek, or from the supply of sandy clay with vegetation debris from which the troughs and pots were made, were fistfuls of clay which were squeezed into struts, or handbricks, to support the trough over the fire in the hearth where the brine was to be evaporated. Sometimes small wedges of clay, squeezed between finger and thumb, were required to correctly balance the trough, or a tier of two or three troughs. The fire, having been lit with brushwood, was stoked with peat where it was available locally, or with turves. As salt crystals began to appear, more brine was poured in until there was sufficient salt to be chopped out when still damp. This was placed in other pottery vessels for the final drying process into convenient 'denominational' salt cakes for trading. The very nature of the processes involved meant that breakages were common, or even necessary to remove the salt (particularly where there had been a quick boiling to produce white, fine grain salt), and the site soon became littered with pottery fragments and unwanted baked strut supports. These would help to build up the hearth for further firings. In time this created a low mound which, if there were a number of hearths together, could be 100 feet or more across. When sifting through this debris, it is interesting to grip the strut and try to determine whether it was a right-hander or a left-hander. An occasional fragment even preserves the actual finger or thumb print of its Iron Age maker.

The industry was widespread in both time and area, with very little relationship to the present coastline. The Wash then was a huge shallow bay of mudflats and marshy islands; the shoreline saltworks were in what is now Helpringham, Rippingale, and Dowsby Fens, 15 miles from the present coast. One of the largest mounds, at Rippingale, grew to five feet in height and about 200 feet across, a sign of considerable industry. On the basis of finds so far made (at least 100 saltern sites are known from this period) the greatest concentration of activity was in the present parishes of Hogsthorpe,

Ingoldmells, Addlethorpe, Orby and Winthorpe. Here streams like the
Burlands and Welton Becks meandered between low hummocks of
boulder clay, which protruded through the marsh clays into tidal
creeks, giving an ideal situation for salt making.
David N. Robinson, The Book of the Lincolnshire Seaside, *(1981), pp.37-38.*

Growing Woad

*Another of Lincolnshire's lost remnants of cultivation was growing
woad, a plant that produced a blue dye.*

One of Lincolnshire's many improving landowners, John Cartwright,
whose radical politics earned him the title of 'the Father of Reform'
and the political dislike of most of his neighbours, built Brotherton
Hall, cultivated woad on a large scale and set up a processing plant on
the North Forty Foot Drain, accompanied by a long row of cottages
for the labourers. The settlement was given the name Isatica after the
Latin name for the plant. It did not survive for long, however,
although woad growing continued at various places in the Fens until
well into the present [twentieth] century.
Michael Lloyd, Portrait of Lincolnshire, *(1983), p. 97.*

Arthur Young, in Agriculture of Lincolnshire, *includes woad in a
chapter on 'Crops not Commonly Cultivated'. He approves of Mr
Cartwright's methods.*

The culture of this plant has been carried to such perfection, on a very
extensive scale By J Cartwright, Esq. at Brothertoft Farm near Boston
that it will be sufficient to explain his management. His father had
been mainly in the old system by moveable colonies, but as the trouble
of that method of conducting the business was considerable, his son
attempted, and successfully, to fix it to one spot. For this purpose it
was necessary, first to secure a tract of land sufficiently large for
affording a certain number of acres annually in crop, for keeping the
buildings and machinery in work, so that the business might go on
with regularity. At Brothertoft he purchased such a tract: so it will be

proper to consider it under the articles of, Soil, Culture and Manufacture to render it saleable.

Soil. – Woad being a tap-rooted plant, penetrating eight or nine inches, of a substantial size, it necessarily demands a deep soil; the best is rich loam; a stiff clay is unfavourable... Experience has proved that the plant thrives best on fresh grassland...

Culture. – In order to bring the woad into a state ready for the dyer's use, it must go through a fermentative process for seven or eight weeks; this is called couching. It is this; the dry balls are taken from the stores and ground to a powder in the same mill and in the same manner as green woad... In respect to the final state of the commodity, Mr Cartwright has found very great advantage in being particularly attentive to the drying and storing it completely for preservation, and which he could affect only by means of the apparatus being well calculated for those purposes... Without these attentions the woad will not beaver well, a term descriptive of the fineness of the capillary filaments into which it draws out when broken between finger and thumb.

Arthur Young, Agriculture of Lincolnshire, *(1808), pp.179-181.*

4 · BY ROAD, RAIL & AIR

Ancient Routes

The highways and byways of the county are mostly very ancient.
Ermine Street, which reaches Stamford from Sussex, drives a straight
course through the county up to the Humber – and is, of course, a
Roman road. So is the Fossway, which coming from Devon, through
Bath and Leicester, enters the county between Newark and Lincoln.
Tillbridge Lane is a smaller Roman road, connecting Ermine Street
with Littleborough and Doncaster, crossing the Trent near Gate
Burton. Many of the byways are very ancient, too, and some, not so
long ago, were but green lanes.

But the Romans gave us not only roads; they gave us canals too;
connecting the Witham at Lincoln and the Trent at Torksey is the
Roman canal called the Fossdyke, which is still extensively used. The
Carr Dyke, which encompasses fifty-seven miles from Peterborough
to Lincoln, is also Roman, but seems to have been formed for
purposes of drainage, rather than for navigation. There are eighteenth
century waterways too, such as the Slea Navigation, which makes its
way, much silted up but in process of recovery, from Sleaford (where
an imposing gateway in Carre Street is entitled Navigation Wharf) to
join the Witham south of Tattershall. Not far upstream, the
Horncastle Navigation joins the Witham here, being a canalised
section of the River Bain. Further north, the Louth Navigation makes
an impressive debut in Louth itself with a grand warehouse and

wharf, to make for the sea at Tetney; but alas this is much silted up. The new river Ancholme took barges for miles south of the Humber, to disembark their valuable cargo at Brandy Wharf, where the great warehouse and a welcoming public house stand solitary and somewhat forlorn beside the Navigation.

Henry Thorold, Lincolnshire, *(1996), pp. 50-51.*

Farmer's Ways

Winding roads are rare in Lincolnshire because they are typical of densely wooded country where the men who made them could not see their goal from any distance. The typical Lincolnshire road runs straight until it takes inexplicable right-angle turns; the goal is clear enough to us but there was some obstacle to earlier travellers that is invisible now. It goes deviously but very soberly, negotiating the layout of open arable fields that have gone: along the side of a furlong, along the headland, and then off again at right-angles. It was not made by men travelling far and anxious to get there, but by farmers with their eyes on the ground, on their neighbours' crops; such men would not commit the discourtesy to a neighbour of taking a short cut. Take a party of country folk in a bus (as I have done) and though they may have expressed a willingness to be shown a notable church or a medieval castle, the real pleasure of the men is in the journey itself, and in the chance to admire good crops and feel superior satisfaction at bad ones. Such men made these roads for their own convenience, and we have inherited in them part of the frame of mind of the countryman.

M.W. Barley, Lincolnshire and the Fens, *(1952), p.20.*

Maintaining the Roads

Until the nineteenth century the roads of Lincolnshire were travelled more by cattle than by people. Imagine the state of them!

The traffic using the roads was insignificant compared with the present day, but they were much frequented by stock. The great herds of highland cattle, estimated at 40,000 beasts in a year, which passed through the county on the way to London markets, must have rendered the roads filthy. In the month of October 1848, some 2,638 animals paid toll at Barton, and over 3,500 at Wrawby. The Turnpike Act of 1764 allowed reduced tolls for Scotch [sic] cattle between Donington and Spalding. The cattle, however, avoided toll bars as much as possible by using grass tracks. Herds of 300, often accompanied by droves of Shetland ponies, swam the Trent at Marton and ate their way southwards. Many pastured in the Fens near Boston much to the indignation of most of the commoners. The inns, like the 'Leeds Gate' at Coningsby, and 'Ferry Boat' at Langrick, offered special accommodation for the drovers. Great droves of geese, too, set off in late summer for the metropolis, feeding on the stubbles as they went. They were 'shod' for the journey by being driven over patches of pitch and sand.

The market towns had their streets paved, and some provision was made for keeping them clean. Caistor was frequently allowed a highway rate in the eighteenth century, and in 1765 two farmers were appointed scavengers at Epworth with a 6d. rate. A rate was allowed also at Gainsborough, although the constable there paid £25 annually out of his rate for cleaning and repairing the streets, and two scavengers were appointed by the court-leet. In 1769 an Act of Parliament was obtained for paving and lighting the streets.

In the eighteenth century the many Parliamentary Enclosures must have caused a great improvement in the roads; at Barton new roads were constructed, eight acres of stone pits allotted for their upkeep, and John Shepherd, the schoolmaster, appointed surveyor. But it was early in the next century that a determined effort was made to improve parish roads. Societies were formed for this express purpose. In 1813 a meeting at the 'Windmill', Alford, passed a resolution to enforce, by indictment at the assizes if necessary, the thorough repair of the public roads within ten miles of the town. The Market Rasen Association employed its own surveyor, and not only enforced the adequate repair of the highway from Langworth through Stainton, Snelland, Wickenby, Lissington, and Linwood to Market Rasen, but also drew attention to the nuisance of seventeen heavy gates erected across the above named road.

Everywhere there was much expenditure on the roads; at Tetney in

1818 over £500 was spent. A great improvement must have followed the adoption of Macadam's 'Instructions for repairing highways'. These are frequently found pasted into the Surveyor's Account books. It seems curious to read, in parishes where stone walls predominate, 'that all hedges must be cut down, which prevent, in the smallest degree, the sun from shining on the road, or obstruct the free circulation of the air'.

Charles Brears, Lincolnshire in the Seventeenth and Eighteenth Centuries, *(1940), pp.94-96.*

The First Railway Line

The first railway in the county was the line opened in 1846 from Lincoln to Nottingham. Two years later, the lines from Sheffield to Grimsby, Grimsby to Peterborough and Lincoln to New Holland via Barnetby were opened. Within a few years most of the present railways had been constructed. Very many more were projected, but as the owner of an estate in Fulbeck stated in opposition to a line proposed from Spalding to Newark, 'the line will pass through a county entirely agricultural, very thinly peopled and almost devoid of traffic'. There was some opposition to the railways from people who disliked 'new-fangled' ways and exorbitant charges were paid before the lines were laid. Although the Manchester, Sheffield and Lincolnshire Company had paid a large sum in tolls when the railway was constructed, the Brigg Turnpike Trustees attempted to compel them to pay for the approaches to the railway. The same company had to pay £17,000 to the freemen of Grimsby for land utilized for the line. At Holton-le-Clay the vestry assessed two miles of railway at £300 per mile to the poor rate, although previously the total assessment of the parish was but £1,565. At Kirton Lindsey in 1846 an attempt was made to make the railway pay for the repair of some of the roads.

Charles Brears, Lincolnshire in the Seventeenth and Eighteenth Centuries, *(1940), p. 184*

The Great Trains

You can sense Henry Thorold's passion for railways as he writes about the opening of the lines and stations in Lincolnshire.

The Great Northern main line from King's Cross reached Grantham in 1852 (there was already a line from Grantham to Nottingham, opened in 1850), and made its way north to Newark, Retford and Doncaster. It is not always realised that the original workshops of the Great Northern Railway were at Boston, and the main line from King's Cross ran through Peterborough and Boston, and thence to Lincoln and Doncaster. This is the way Queen Victoria went to Balmoral in 1851. It is hard to imagine those main line trains pursuing the somewhat tortuous line that until a few years ago accompanied the River Witham all the way from Boston to Lincoln, past Langrick and Tattershall, Stixwould and Bardney. The fact was that the more direct route, via Grantham, Newark and Retford (which came to be known as the Towns Line), owing to the steep gradients between Peterborough and Grantham), had not been built. This did not open until 1852. Boston had two years of glory.

Until very recently there survived many of the old buildings of the Great Northern Railway workshops here at Boston. But everything is gone now. Boston is merely the end (or nearly the end) of a branch line from Grantham and Sleaford. One thing survives, and that recently and most handsomely restored, the railway station itself, with its imposing portico – an altogether delightful building as so many of these mid-nineteenth-century railway buildings are.

But even after 1852 Boston was still the centre of an important railway network, with lines to Lincoln and Grimsby to the north, to Spalding, Peterborough and London to the south, shortly to be linked to Sleaford and Grantham to the west, and to Wainfleet and Skegness to the east. The greatest trains of all went through Grantham, along the grand new Great Northern Line. It has been the author's pleasure and privilege to live for much of his life within a mile of this line, within sight of these great trains. Indeed, for several miles the line was built across the family estate, and when young he would often walk with his father to the Frinkley Lane crossing to watch the Flying Scotsman or the Queen of Scots, the Silver Jubilee (1935), or The

Coronation (1937) flash by.

The other great Lincolnshire line was the East Lincolnshire Railway which ran from Grimsby to Boston, and again was one of the earliest railways in the county. There had been for some years great interest in the idea of building a line parallel with the Lincolnshire coast, and Parliament authorised the scheme in 1846.

Henry Thorold, Lincolnshire, (1996), pp. 52-53.

The Coming of the Railway

David Steel tells how the railway affected the lives of the people living in Corby, a village that later added Glen, the name of a nearby river, to distinguish it from the steel town of Corby in Northamptonshire.

The long-term effects on rural communities of the arrival of the railway system, linking up the countryside with distant job and recreational opportunities and helping to bring new goods and ideas into the countryside cannot be too strongly stressed. The construction of the lines also had short-term effects which have been less closely studied. Luckily the 1851 census catches within its net, like some engulfing purse skeine, the builders of the 'Towns Line' of the Great Northern Railway. The stretch, opened in July 1852, connected Peterborough, Grantham and Newark directly with the north.

In Corby parish in 1851 there were 106 railwaymen with their families. What effect did such men have on the countryside through which the lines were being constructed? The immediate effect of railway construction was in the use of raw materials. Lord Willoughby's steward, for instance, went to Grantham timber yard to find out what price could be obtained for elm, and contracts followed for the supply of sleepers and sand. The dependence of purely local materials should not be exaggerated, however. When Lord Willoughby built his own railway from Little Bytham to Edenham, the steward was sent to Hull and Grimsby to buy Baltic timber.

The effects of railway construction were greatest on the immediate communities through which the lines pass. As early contracts relied almost entirely on men with picks and shovels, the work did indeed call for the strong men depicted in the idea of the mythical navvy. But as the railway labourers' wages in the year 1851 were at the lowest for the whole period 1843 to 1869, the contractors at Corby could pick and choose from those who sought employment. Owing to the existence of this pool of labour, they would be unlikely to take on raw recruits from the countryside. For his part the countryman, even with his low wage of about 12s a week, might not have found the shoveller's wage of 14s a week so much more attractive than his 12s and any perks he received with this.

An analysis of the railway workers living at Corby and neighbouring Burton [Coggles] shows that hardly any were from the immediate vicinity although 17 and 13 per cent respectively were from Kesteven. Almost exactly one third were from Lincolnshire ... Of the 145 men at Burton, only 15 were from large towns, whilst there were 7 from the Lincolnshire village of Pinchbeck alone.

Although the majority of railway builders were new to the Corby area there is no evidence that they were not integrated into the community, where they would have provided a welcome addition to many a family's income. Here again, they kept very close to their place of work. In Burton, where the railway population was large in comparison with the available housing, more than half the workers lived in huts, each looked after by one of the men and his wife. Another nineteen men were living in the barn of an inn, which had been fitted out as a dormitory

David I. A. Steel, A Lincolnshire Village, *(1979), pp.169 - 171.*

Solving the Problem

At the beginning of the last century the roads were in such a poor state that travelling at times was almost impossible. W.F. Rawnsley tells the story of an ingenious farmer.

A few years ago, when the first motor made its way into Lincolnshire, the road from Gainsborough to Louth was one long stretch of small, loose stones. It had never even dreamt of a steam roller, and there were always ruts for the wheels, and as Lincolnshire carriage wheels were set three or four inches wider apart so that they could accommodate themselves to the cart ruts, when we brought a carriage up from Oxfordshire it was found impossible to use it till the axles had been cut and lengthened so that it could run in the ruts. But this was a great improvement on the days my grandmother remembered, when it took four stout horses to draw a carriage at a foot's pace from Ingoldmells to Spilsby (and this was only 100 years ago), or when Sir Charles Anderson saw a small cart-load of corn stuck on the road and thatched down for the winter there, doubtless belonging to a small farmer who had but one horse, which could not draw the load home.

W.F. *Rawnsley,* Highways and Byways of Lincolnshire, *(1914), p. 207.*

Setting the Scene

This first excerpt from Lincolnshire Airfields in the Second World War *by Patrick Otter has a real sense of what the county must have been like during the war. Names like Scampton, Coningsby and Waddington will forever be associated with the heroism of the aircrews of Bomber Command, who night after night took off across the Fens and headed out over the North Sea. The second piece is by Guy Gibson, who was born in Lincolnshire.*

You have to look closely these days for the evidence but half a century ago Lincolnshire was at the very heart of Britain's air power. Now the markers are hard to find. A distant view of a hangar roof, now perhaps a warehouse or a grain depot; a crumbling building in the corner of a wheat field; a stretch of unexplained concrete; the hump back of a rotting Nissen hut; the overgrown ribs of what might have been an air raid shelter. Then there are the memorials to the men and machines which packed into this green backwater of England between 1939 and 1945. They range from simple roadside plaques to the dramatic memorial at Woodhall Spa to the country's most famous airmen of all, the Dambusters.

So many airfields were to be found in the country's second largest county that it was estimated that there was, on average, only seven miles between each of them. They covered an estimated 30,000 acres of Lincolnshire, accommodating around 80,000 RAF personnel at any one time. Big though Lincolnshire skies are, the county was so crowded with military airfields that circuits overlapped and flying operations had to be curtailed in the Lincoln area. At the peak of wartime aviation, there were some 46 military airfields plus numerous ancillary sites in the county. Now that figure has shrunk to a handful with only two, Coningsby and Waddington, still operational.

When the surveyors began looking for new sites for airfields, they were not drawn to the flat fenlands around the Wash, but to the rolling farmlands of the Lincolnshire Cliff, the fertile plain south of Lincoln and the uplands on the edge of the Wolds. It was here that most of the county's wartime airfields were to be found.

It is easy to see why these areas were chosen. Sites along the cliff (as a geographic description, this is not strictly accurate; it is a natural limestone escarpment, but its steep, west-facing edge earned it the name 'cliff' long before the RAF came) were well drained and sat astride the Ermine Street, the main arterial road through Lincolnshire. The farmland south of Lincoln was well drained and free from obstruction while the Wolds sites, some of which were over 400 feet above sea level, were able to make full use of the prevailing south-westerly winds.

By quirk of planning and geography, the city of Lincoln found itself at the hub of an almost complete circle of airfields. There were some 16 airfields within a ten mile radius of the city centre (including Wigsley, just across the county boundary in Nottinghamshire). So crowded did the sky become at one stage that a Lancaster squadron had to be moved to an airfield to the east of the county to relieve the congestion. Circuits still overlapped to such an extent that one airfield, Dunholme Lodge, eventually closed for operational flying.

The airfields themselves ranged from the very good pre-war stations to the jerry-built wartime-only ones. Not all the wartime-built airfields were bad, but most were. Accommodation was Spartan, mostly in Nissen huts where the only running water was supplied by leaking roofs or condensation. Most were without electricity and all had just a single coke stove to keep the occupants warm. Medical officers issued dire warnings about the threat of illness and disease while, outside, hastily laid concrete runways broke up under the weight of aircraft using them.

Patrick Otter, Lincolnshire Airfields in the Second World War, *(1996) pp. 9, 12-13.*

Flight Out

The moon was full; everywhere its pleasant, watery haze spread over the peaceful English countryside, rendering it colourless. But there is not much colour in Lincolnshire, anyway. The city of Lincoln was silent – that city which so many bomber boys know so well, a city full of homely people. People who have got so used to the Air Force that they have begun to almost forget them. Lincoln, with its great cathedral sticking up on a hill, a landmark for miles around. Little villages in the flat Fenland slept peacefully. Here nice, simple folk live in their bastions on the East Anglian coast. The last farmer had long since gone to bed, the fire in the village pub had died down to an ember. The bar, which a few hours ago was full of noisy, chattering people, was silent. There were no enemy aircraft about and the scene was peaceful. In fact, this sort of scene might not have changed for a hundred years or so. But this night was different – at least for 133 men: 133 young fliers, and I was one of those men. This was the big thing. This was it.

We were flying not very high, about one hundred feet, and not very far apart. I suppose to a layman it was a wonderful sight, these great powerful Lancasters in formation, flown by boys who knew their job. Below us, and also practically beside us, at 200 miles an hour flashed past trees, fields, church spires and England.

We were off on a journey for which we had long waited, a journey that had been carefully planned, carefully trained for, a mission that was going to do a lot of good if it succeeded; and everything had been worked out so that it should succeed. We were off to the Dams.

Those who have seen a Lancaster cockpit in the light of the moon, flying just above the earth, will know what I mean when I say it is very hard to describe. The pilot sits on the left of a raised comfortably padded seat fitted with arm rests. He usually flies the thing with his left hand, re-setting the gyro and other instruments with his right, but most pilots use both hands when over enemy territory or when the going is tough. You have to be quite strong to fly a Lancaster.

In front of him the instruments sit winking. On the sperry panel, or the blind-flying panel as bomber pilots call it, now and then a red light, indicating that some mechanism needs adjusting, will suddenly flash on. The pilot of a bomber must know everything. He must know the duties of the rest of the crew inside out, and should be able to take any one of them over should the occasion arise. The flight-engineer is the pilot's mate and sits beside him watching the engine instruments. Most flight-engineers were ground mechanics of bomber command who have volunteered to fly on operations, and a grand job of work they do, too.

It is warm inside and both pilot and flight-engineer are very lightly clad, their oxygen masks hanging on one strap from the corner of the face. These masks are necessary evils. When over enemy territory they are worn continuously, not only because oxygen is required but because the pilot has no time to take his hand off the wheel and put the microphone up to his face. The result is that one gets quite chapped after six hours with the ting on. Many times the question is asked, "Why can't we have throat microphones like the Americans?"

Between the two front windows is a large instrument, perhaps the most important of all, the repeating compas, worked by a master unit at the back. The pilot's eyes constantly perform a non-stop circle from the repeater to the A.S.I [air speed indicator], from the A.S.I. to the horizon, from the horizon to the moon, from the moon to what he can see on the ground and then back to the repeater. No wonder they are red-rimmed when he returns.

Such is the scene. The glass house. Soft moonlight. Two silent figures, young, unbearded, new to the world yet full of skill, full of pride in their squadron, determined to do a good job and bring the ship home. A silent scene, whose only incidental music is provided by the background hiss of air and the hearty roar of four Merlin engines. *Wing-Commander Guy Gibson, V.C., D.S.O., D.F.C., Enemy Coast Ahead, (1946), pp. 17 – 18.*

The Last Mission

Twenty thousand feet beneath the Lancaster lay the city, naked and vulnerable, trapped in the faint moonbeams of the winter night. The sky, ablaze with the lancing brilliance of wheeling searchlights, was draped with lethal curtains of heavy flak bursting like blossom around them.

Skip, a hardened veteran of 59 raids, kept the aircraft cruising in the safe zone of darkness, immediately above the point where the searching beams had converged on a bomber, now being relentlessly pounded by ground defences. Caught like a moth in the coning shafts of light, there could be no escape. Wings ablaze, the doomed plane spiralled to earth like a fiery cross, impacting the ground with a sickening thud and spilling shooting orange flames into the raging holocaust.

Skip was listening for the command from the master bomber circling somewhere above him. When it came he began the bombing run, flying straight into the hostile sky, the moment feared by all members of the crew, their stomach muscles taught with fear, faces drawn and grey with tension. The gunners watched the coloured balls of tracer raking past the wing tips, and fired down the beams.

Ahead lay the marker flare shining a vivid scarlet, unmistakable amid the smoke and flame. 'Bombs gone,' announced the bomb-aimer laconically and released the photo-flash. As he watched the flicker of exploding bombs the plane suddenly dived, sliding down the sky to avoid the probing fingers of light. Banking steeply, it retreated swiftly into the cover of darkness.

The roar of the Merlin died to a comforting whisper as the aircraft joined the main bomber stream heading for base, guided by the slow-falling parachute flares. Homeward droned the battle fleet, a thousand heavy bombers, condensation trails streaming out behind them like banners of a victorious army. Mid-upper and rear turrets were swinging as the gunners, eyes alert and watchful, prepared for possible attacks by enemy fighters which followed the drawn-out contrails.

There was the sudden glint of moonlight on metal. The stars were blotted out by a diving black shadow as a Junkers 88 came in from the dark edge of the sky. Cannon shells ripped into the fuselage. In reply the Brownings rattled on their mountings, as the gunners methodically hosed the blackness.

The pilot began corkscrewing the plane, climbing, diving, banking to the left and right in an attempt to shake off the marauder. Slowly the rudder bar responded to his strong pressure and the aircraft gained and the aircraft gained height steadily, the powerful beat of the engines having a reassuring effect on the crew.

'Radio smashed,' commented Ops. 'Lost contact with base.' Skip acknowledged and ordered the navigator to plot a course for the Wash.

Above them, starlight and friendly moon glittered in a frosty, metallic sky. Below, the shimmering expanse of the North Sea stretched away to a shadowy horizon.

Slowly small wisps of cloud began to form and drift across the sky., building up into banks of thick, grey mist, dank and impenetrable. Flecks of icy rain hissed past the fuselage, blurring the Perspex and blinding the crew. The rising wind moaned eerily, savagely buffeting the lost aircraft, now but a tiny, floating world alone in a vast, illimitable emptiness.

The men lapsed into silence, despair in their hearts. An increasing feeling of isolation filled their minds, a sense of timelessness as if they had flown into another dimension where boundaries had no existence. The cold had become so intense; the silence so deep; the darkness so complete.

Confused images of the night's raid clouded the mind of the rear gunner, as, stiff and exhausted he crouched in the narrow confines of his turret. 'The last operation of the tour, too,' he thought in bitter frustration.

Flight checked the fuel gauges and concealed his anxiety.

Suddenly there was a loud bang near the port wing, followed by anti-aircraft shells exploding in a sea of fire round them. The British coastal defences were taking no chances. Skip looked grim and took the aircraft up two thousand feet. Remembering the day, he muttered a quiet prayer.

As if in answer to his clumsy words the mist was pierced by a dazzling radiance which filled the sky, catching the towers of Lincoln Cathedral far below in brilliant rays of light. Moonlight bathed the sleeping city in a delicate, sliver sheen.

Few people were astir that Sunday morning. The streets lay quiet and empty, but already a faint flush of gold had appeared in the eastern sky. Inside the cathedral, communicants knelt before the altar, conscious of the pulsating throb of the returning bomber's engines.

The plane banked, altering course to fly the last few miles to base. Soon the winking lights of the flare-path were sighted. Skip, his face haggard with weariness, but his mind filled with a sense of elation, touched the Lancaster gently down on the runway to complete the last mission.

Tom Herbert, Lincolnshire Life, *April 1982, pp38-39*

5 · SPORTS AND PASTIMES

Tales of Past Sports

In most villages there are traditional sporting events that take place throughout the year. Many of them gradually died out as people became more aware of the cruelty involved, but they were once part of village life and the village year. David Steel writes about some of the country sports that were popular in Corby Glen.

There is no folk memory of cock-fighting in the old Fighting Cocks Inn although what may have been a cockpit was filled in about the turn of this century [twentieth]. Stories, however, of prize-fighting have been passed down and whippet-racing, organised by the landlord of the Wheatsheaf, can be remembered.

At the end of the nineteenth century the point-to-point races at Ingoldsby, at which Colonel Paravacini, later of the Birkeholme, was a successful participant, were popular with the people of Corby. The fleet-footed bookies, the county people with their servants and the free lunch for farmers who allowed the hounds to go over their land are all remembered.

George Bird himself also took part in sporting events in Corby, such as Mr Pawley's coursing party on which the *Grantham Journal* reported. A party of gentlemen had met at Heath's Railway Hotel for coursing and twenty sat down for dinner afterwards, Mr Pawley presiding. The coursing parties were held in February. At the end of the year there was sometimes pigeon-shooting. Here, again, gambling played a part. Bird recalled one such occasion thus: Mr Paling had his annual pigeon-shooting, I was book-keeper. I had my dinner with the company, not so many crackshots as last year, not so much betting going on as in former years.

Participation in such sports as horse-racing or pigeon-shooting was confined to those who could afford the necessary equipment. Of, perhaps, greater significance for the rural communities was the development of clubs for cricket and, later, football. In the 1850s cricket became organised on a local, county and all-England basis.
David I. A. Steel, A Lincolnshire Village, *(1979), p. 186.*

No Games on Sunday

The spread of Puritanism during the seventeenth century meant that many spare time activities were frowned upon, and positively discouraged on the Sabbath.

Sports and amusements on the Sabbath were curtailed. In 1606 the churchwardens of Pinchbeck were in trouble for allowing stoolball play on the Sabbath. Later it was complained that Mr Holt, parson at Stamford All Saints', had allowed stoolball to be played on Sundays in the street near his own door and in the church yard; while Thomas Gibson, Vicar of Horncastle, had many times on the Lord's Day gone shooting in the afternoon, and had urged his neighbours to do the like. Some games were prohibited by manorial by-laws, such as football at Kirton Lindsey and quoits at Ingoldmells. Although the gentry had bowling greens at Driby and Ancaster, the game was forbidden by statute to ordinary people. This did not prevent the people of Grimsby from indulging in the game, and also from playing cards, which was also illegal. In 1575 the parson of Elkington was charged with playing at card tables and dice.

Field sports were very popular among the wealthy, especially deer hunting, coursing for hares, hawking and horse racing. Sir William Pelham, writing to his father-in-law, Lord Conway, described their hawking at Broughton. 'Exercise is the best physic ... The hawk failed of her part, yet there were many passages which made amends. Mr Anderson with violent running almost burst himself.'

Partridges were the usual quarry for hawks, but the number of wildfowl reared in the mews at Brocklesby for hawking was prodigious. There were horse races at Grantham, Lincoln and Grimsby and no doubt in other places too. In 1609 Sir John Sheffield bought for £140 a Barbary horse at Marseilles.

When James I approached Lincoln from Grantham in 1617, he did not keep to the highway but hunted over the Heath. He was so much in love with the country about Lincoln that he made up his mind to spend part of his winters there. In the city he was entertained by a horse race, a hunt, a foot race and a fencing match. At the sign of the George by the Stonebow he had four cocks put in the pit together, which made his majesty very merry.

Charles Brears, Lincolnshire in the Seventeenth and Eighteenth Centuries, *(1940), p.20-21.*

Stamford Bull-Running

This 'gallant sport,' according to tradition, originated thus: – in the reign of King John two bulls fighting on the meadow were parted by a butcher, when one of the animals ran into the town, where, chased and infuriated by dogs, it tossed men women and children. Earl Warren, seeing from the castle what was going on, mounted his horse and rode after the bull. Tickled at the fun, he gave the meadow to the butchers of the town on condition they for ever provided a bull to be run annually on the 13th of November. But it has been appositely observed that, Hokday, the anniversary of the massacre of the Danes, being chosen for the baiting, there was probably some connection between it and the commemoration of a national event, as the Danish and English castles here confronted each other.

The mode of pursuing the sport in the time of Charles I is described by a writer of the period – 'In the morning the proclamation is made by the common bellman that each one shut up their shop doors and gates; that none under pain of imprisonment offer violence to strangers; and that none have iron upon their bull-clubs. Which proclamation made and the town gates closed, the bull – the wildest the butchers can procure – is turned out of the Alderman's stable, and then hivie skivy, tag and rag, men, women, and children (with all the dogs in the town) running after him, with their bull-clubs spattering dirt in each others faces, that one would think them to be so many Furies started out of Hell for the punishment of Cerberus'.

Within the memory of men I knew the proceedings were much the same. At the public-houses and at other convivial assemblies in the town for six weeks before and six weeks after the Taurine festival it was customary for men to sing the glories of the sport. The vehicle for the expression, if not for the strengthening, of the popular sentiment was a rude doggrel in keeping with the coarseness of the diversion itself. This, known as 'The Bullards' Song,' is printed in *Old Lincolnshire*, together with the lively music.

On the morning of the eventful day the bell of St Mary's tolled for the thoroughfares to be cleared of children and the infirm (it sometimes, too, rang out the knell of a fated reveller), spectators crowded the windows and housetops, bold athletes stood below on tip-toe of expectation, and then out bounced the bull. Teased into fury to afford prime sport, the beast would test to the utmost the watchfulness and agility of the bullards, and many an unfortunate 'runner,' caught ere he gained a cask round which those hard pressed might manoeuvre, would be shot into the air to descend to the music of the multitude. One great object was to 'bridge' the bull, i.e., pitch him over the parapet into the Welland, and if this feat were accomplished by noon the butchers had to provide another bull.

Sometimes to goad it into a frenzy, men would gash the flesh of a tame, inoffensive animal, and apply vitriol to the gaping wounds. At one time, it was customary after the running to chain the poor beast to a peg and bait it with dogs. In the evening the friendly axe would come to the rescue, and the tormentors would end their orgies with a supper of 'bull beef.' In addition to the November celebration there would occasionally be a 'stop' running, i.e., confined to a particular street. In 1776 the landlord of the Half Moon public-house entertained the inhabitants with one of these, when 'there was good sport, many persons being tossed and gored, and one man having an eye knocked out.' The bull bolted into the kitchen of the inn: some of the customers ascended the chimney, others escaped through the window, and one or two found refuge under the table. The practice was regarded with favour by others than trade-driving publicans.

In 1737 at the vestry of St George's it was agreed 'that the churchwardens for the future be allowed at the bull-running yearly 10s.for their expenses, and no more.' Mr Robert Ridlington, Mayor of Stamford in1756, left half-a-crown annually to each of the parishes for the trouble of stopping the gates and avenues to the town during this 'riot feast'. Indeed, in the early part of the 19th century aspirants to Parliamentary honours won the poorer electors more readily by promising a bull than by bribery in other forms; and as late as 1831 would-be hon. members started on their canvass under a banner displaying a picture of the beast. Some humane spirits, however, had long ago raised their voices. In 1788 the Magistrates attempted to suppress bull-running, but they were roughly handled by the mob. The following year a detachment of Dragoons sent to support the civil power fraternized with the people. Opposition subsiding, the bullards kept on their course' but in 1833 so little interest was taken in the sport that, despite the wiles of the blue-frocked 'bull-woman' (a personage who made it her duty to collect subscriptions), it was with difficulty that money could be raised to buy or hire a bull.

Yet official efforts to stamp out the embers developed the latent love. On the morning of the 13th Nov., 1839, the Mayor and Magistrates assembled at the Town-hall, a force of metropolitan police was in attendance, special constables were called out, a detachment of the 5th Dragoons mounted guard at the George, and horse patrols scoured the neighbourhood with orders to give instant notice should Taurus be seen approaching. At noon the cry of 'Bull! Bull!' was roared from a thousand throats. A steer labelled 'for Stamford' had been adroitly introduced. It escaped into the fields, and was chased to Tolethorpe, where it took to the river. On the banks bullard and bluecoat fought for possession, but the soldiery soon trotted up, and the 'bull', between files of Dragoons and a posse of police, and amid the excrations of the people, was led to safe quarters in the town. This little luxury cost the ratepayers £300, so they vowed to the Secretary of State that they would run no more bulls, and the vow has been faithfully kept.

George H. Burton, Stamford Bull-Running, *(1927), pp.2-7.*

The Decoys

In his journey through England and Wales at the beginning of the eighteenth century, Daniel Defoe was clearly fascinated by the use of decoy or duckoy ducks in Lincolnshire. Here he describes, quite dramatically, how the decoys were trained to lure other ducks to their downfall.

The art of taking the fowls, and especially of breeding up a set of creatures, call'd decoy ducks, to entice and then betray their fellow-ducks into the several decoys, is very admirable indeed, and deserves a description; tho' 'tis not very easy to describe it, take it in as few words as I can.

The decoy ducks are first naturalised to the place, for they are hatch'd and bred up in the decoy ponds. There are in the ponds certain places where they are constantly fed, and where being made tame, they are used to come even to the decoy man's hand for their food.

When they fly abroad, or, as might be said, are sent abroad, they go none knows where, but 'tis believ'd by some they fly quite over the seas in Holland and Germany. There they meet with others of their acquaintance, that is to say, of their own kind, where sorting with them, and observing how poorly they live, how all the rivers are frozen up, and the lands cover'd with snow, and that they almost starv'd, they fail not to let them know, (in language that they make one another understand) that in England, from whence they came, the case is quite alter'd; that the English ducks live much better than they do in those cold climates, that they have open lakes, and sea shores full of food, the tides flowing freely into every creek. That they have also within the land, large lakes, refreshing springs of water, open ponds, covered and secured from human eyes, with large rows of grown trees and impenetrable groves. That the lands are full of food, the stubbles yielding constant supplies of corn, left by negligent husbandmen, as it were on purpose for their use, that 'tis not once in a wild duck's age. That they have long frosts or deep snows, and that when they have, yet the sea is never frozen, or the shores void of food;

and that if they will please but go with them into England, they share with them in all these good things.

By these representations, made in their own duck language (or by whatever other arts which we know not) they draw together a vast number of fowls, and, in a word, kidnap them from their own country; for once being brought out of their knowledge, they follow the decoys, as long as a dog follows the huntsman; and 'tis frequent to see these subtle creatures return with a vast flight of fowls with them, or at their heels, as we may say, after the said decoy ducks have been absent several weeks together.

When they have brought them over, the first thing they do is to settle with them in the decoy ponds, to which they (the decoy ducks) belong. Here they chatter and gabble to them, in their own language, as if they were telling them, that these are the ponds they told them of, and here they should soon see how well they should live, how secure and how safe a retreat they had here.

When the decoy-men perceive they are come, and that they are gathering and encreasing (sic), they fail not to go secretly to the pond's side, I say secretly, and under the cover which they have made with reeds, so that they cannot be seen, where they throw over the reeds handfuls of corn, in shallow places, such where the decoy ducks are usually fed, and where they are sure to come for it, and to bring their new guests with them for their entertainment.

This they do for two or three days together, and no harm follows, 'till throwing in this bait one time in an open wide place, another time in another open wide place, the third time it is thrown in a narrower place; that is to say where the trees hang over the water and the banks, stand nearer, and then in another yet narrower, where the said trees are overhead like an arbour, though at a good hight [sic] from the water.

Here the boughs area artfully managed, that a large net is spread near the tops of the trees among the branches, and fasten'd to hoops which reach from side to side. This is so high and so wide, and the room is so much below, and the water so open, that the fowls do not perceive the net above them at all.

Here the decoy-man keeping unseen, behind the hedges of reeds, which are made perfectly close, goes forward, throwing corn over the reeds into the water. The decoy ducks greedily fall upon it, and calling their foreign guests, seem to tell them, that now they may find their words good, and how well the ducks live in England; so inviting or rather wheedling them forward, 'till by degrees they are all gotten under the arch or sweep of the net, which is on the trees, and which by degrees, imperceptibly to them, declines lower and lower, and also narrower and narrower, 'till

at the farther end it comes to a point like a purse; though this farther end is quite out of sight, and perhaps two or three hundred yards from the first entrance.

When the whole quantity are thus greedily following the leading ducks or decoys, and feeding plentifully as they go, and the decoy-man sees they are all within the arch of the net, and so far within as not to be able to escape, on a sudden a dog, which 'till then he keeps close by him, and who is perfectly taught his business, rushes from behind the reeds, and jumps into the water, swimming directly after the ducks, and (terribly to them) barking as he swims.

Immediately the ducks (frighted to the last degree) rise upon the wing to make their escape, but to their great surprize [sic], are beaten down again by the arched net, which is over their heads. Being then forced into the water, they necessarily swim forward, for fear of that terrible creature the dog; and thus they crowd on, 'till by degrees the net growing lower and narrower, as is said, they are hurried to the very farther end, where another decoy-man stands ready to receive them, and who takes them out alive with his hands.

As for the traytors that drew the poor ducks into this snare, they are taught to rise but a little way, and so not reaching to the net, they fly back to the ponds, and make their escape; or else, being used to the decoy-man, they go to him fearless, and are taken out as the rest; but instead of being kill'd with them, are strok'd, made much of, and put into a little pond just by him, and fed and made much of for their services.

Daniel Defoe, A Tour Through England and Wales, *(1724) vol.2, pp.98-100.*

The Haxey Hood Game

This is a famous tale and found in many variations in books on Lincolnshire. It is worth including in this one.

The sixth of January, being Epiphany or Old Christmas day, is famous in the Isle of Axholme for the throwing of the hood, better known as 'Haxey Hood', the obscure village of Haxey being the scene of this ancient custom, the origin of which is lost in antiquity, though Peck, the historian of the Isle, conjectures that the Mowbrays, the ancient lords of the manor, may have inspired the sport.

The 'Hood', twelve 'Boggons', and a 'Fool' are requisite for the game. The 'Boggons' are twelve men attired in red jackets and the 'Fool' is a species of a rudely-costumed Harlequin. A piece of sacking, about two feet in length, is folded until it is about three inches in diameter, and, being securely tied, forms the famous 'Hood'.

Tradition supplies a very probable origin of the sport. An old lady was traversing the open fields one long-past and windy Twelfth Day when her hood was caught by the wind and sent spinning over the field. A number of worthy villagers gave chase, and recovered the stray hood after some fun and excitement, which the old lady seems to have appreciated, for she bestowed half-an-acre of land in the open Haxey fields upon twelve men, the original 'Boggons', for the purpose of an annual celebration of the fun. The 'Boggons' of today have to content themselves with the fun; their half-acres of land are purely traditional.

The 'Boggons' go round the villages about a week before the throwing of the Hood, and, with merriment and song, invite the rustics to attend the sport and also to assist them with gifts of beer and money.

The sport takes place in the open fields and the 'Boggons' endeavour to prevent the Hood being carried off the field, while the players as strenuously strive to carry it to one of the public-houses in the locality.

At one o'clock the players muster by the churchyard, when the 'Fool', perching upon a large stone, holds forth about 'Hoos agean Hoos, an' Toon agean Toon' and proclaims the quantity of drink offered by the various publicans to the person who carries the Hood to their houses.

The speech over, a rush is made for the fields, where the eldest 'Boggon', styled the 'lord', takes the Hood, and, when the 'Boggons' have taken their places, throws it up. A scene of wild excitement ensues, and if a 'Boggon' succeeds in catching the Hood, he carries it to the 'lord', who, from the middle of the fields, again throws it among the players. The rustics throw the Hood to each other and endeavour to carry it from the field; the 'Boggons' as fiercely strive to keep it within bounds, and if they succeed in carrying their point until evening closes in, they retire and the contest assumes another form, the players contending against each other as to the public-house to which it is to be carried. That point decided, the Hood is roasted before the fire and well basted with ale amid the noisy merriment of the revellers.

The village does not calm down for a day or two, the players parading about to collect gifts of money, beer and corn, after which they begin 'smoking the Fool' at Burnham. A fire of damp straw, etc., is made beneath the branches of a large tree, and the 'Fool' sitting in a loop formed in a stout rope, is suspended from one of the limbs of the tree and is let down into the dense, choking smoke again and again, to the infinite gratification of the rustics. The 'smoking of the Fool' is repeated at Haxey and Westwoodside, and the frolic is wound up by a few nights of wild carousing, after which the Hood is laid aside until Twelfth Mass comes round again and the 'Boggons', 'Fool' and rustics take the field.

William Andrews, Bygone Lincolnshire, *vol 1, (1891), pp. 197-200.*

Fen Skating

The Fen Skaters of Lincolnshire have been famous for centuries. In the Peterborough museum you may see two bone skates made from the shin bones of an ox and a deer ground to a smooth flat surface on one side and pierced at either end with holes, or grooved, for attachment thongs. The regular fen skates, which are only now being ousted by the more convenient modern form, were like the Dutch skates of Teniers' pictures; long, projecting blades twice as long as a man's foot, turned up high at the end and cut off square at the heel. They were called 'Whittlesea runners' and were supposed to be the best form of skate for pace straight ahead; and no man who lived in Ramsey 100 to 200 years ago, or at Peterborough or Croyland was without a pair. The writer has been on Cowbit Wash (pronounced Cubbit), near Spalding, when the great frozen plain was in places black with the crowds of Lincolnshire fenmen, mostly agricultural labourers, all on skates and all thoroughly enjoying themselves, whilst ever and anon a course was cleared, and with a swish of the sounding 'pattens' a couple of men came racing down the long lane bordered with spectators with both arms swinging in time to the long, vigorous strokes which is the fenman's style. The most remarkable thing about the gathering was the splendid physique of the crowd. Could they all have been taken and drilled for military service they would have made a regiment of which Peter the Great would have been proud.

Whatever year you take you will find that the prize-winners for fen skating come from the same district and the same villages; Welney, Whaplode, Gedney, Cowbit and Croyland are perpetually recurring names, the last four being all situated in the south-eastern corner of Lincolnshire which abuts on the Wash between the outfall of the Welland and the Nene.

In the severe frost of 1912, which lasted from January 29 to February 5, the thermometer on the night of February 3 going down to zero, Cowbit Wash saw the contest for both the professional and amateur championship for Lincolnshire.

Willingham Franklin Rawnsley, Highways and Byways of Lincolnshire, *(1914), pp. 405-407.*

The Lincolnshire Fox-hounds

Except the Fen country and a small corner of the extreme north-west, the whole of Lincolnshire is hunted by fox-hounds. Four packs, namely, the Brocklesby (Lord Yarborough's), the Burton, Blankney and Southwold hunt entirely in Lincolnshire; while the Belvoir and Cottesmore hunt partly in Lincolnshire. Premier position must be given to the Brocklesby. It is one of the very few packs maintained entirely by the master, and for over 150 years the earls of Yarborough have done this for the benefit of residents and farmers in the large

tract of country they hunt over. The country hunted extends from the
Humber on the north to a line drawn from Louth to Market Rasen on
the south, and from the sea on the east to the river Ancholme on the
west. The country is mostly wold and consequently plough, but very
open and only big woods being those around Brocklesby itself. The
hounds having been so long in one family are of the best, and there
are few kennels in England but have a large infusion of the Brocklesby
blood, famous for nose, tongue and stoutness. For upwards of 100
years the family of Smith carried the horn and did much to establish
the notoriety of the pack, while in more recent years Will Dale, a great
huntsman and houndsman, and Jem Smith, no relation to the former
huntsman, have kept it up. Possibly sport in the county was never
better than when W. Dale and Mr. Maunsell-Richardson each hunted
one pack; when one was hunting the other was always out to render
assistance, as both knew the country perfectly, the result was more
good runs and more foxes caught at the end of them than was ever
done in the country before or since.

W.F. *Rawnsley*, Highways and Byways of Lincolnshire, *(1914), pp. 493-494.*

Spalding Gentlemen's Society

*This eminent society is almost too grand to include in chapter on
sports and pastimes but it was, and still is, an important part of life in
Spalding and the surrounding area. These days the society admits
women.*

At the very commencement of the eighteenth century, a number of
gentlemen interested in antiquarian pursuits were in the habit of
meeting weekly in London at various coffee-houses in the vicinity of
the Temple. At one of these places Maurice Johnson was introduced
by John Gay, the poet, to Pope, Addison, Steele and other learned
men. The *Tatler* was here read and discussed, but one of the principle
subjects for discussion seems to have been the resuscitation of the
London Society of Antiquaries. It was then agreed that, so soon as
sufficient funds should be obtained, a start should be made. Among
other arrangements, Maurice Johnson was designated its first
librarian.

Johnson, however, having completed his studies and been admitted a member of the Inner Temple, removed to his native town of Spalding.

Born in this town (baptized June 26, 1688), a member of a very influential family in Lincolnshire, he soon met with several professional and other appointments. These led him into the society of many eminent men. He also continued in touch with his friends in London, and retained his love for antiquarian pursuits.

In 1709 he took up his residence in Spalding, and the same year married Elizabeth, daughter of Joseph Ambler, and granddaughter of Anthony Oldfield, who was lineally descended from Sir Thomas Gresham. He, perforce, exchanged the society of the wits of Buttons' Coffee-house and of antiquaries at the Temple 'Change, for the ordinary society of a small country town.

So great, however, was his love of learning and science that he at once entertained the bold design of establishing a literary society in the very heart of the Fens of Lincolnshire. It was, as he very truly said, 'an endeavour new and untried before.' Those to whom he looked for assistance 'were unaccustomed to such a mode of spending an evening'. He took care not to alarm the country gentlemen by premature mention of antiquities, but endeavoured to allure them into the more flowery paths of literature . . .

According to the Society's book-plate, which was engraved by George Vertue, after a design submitted to him by Maurice Johnson, the date of the institution of the Society is 1710. This date is also frequently referred to by the founder as that of its institution . . .

In 1715-16 a little room in the old part of the parsonage-house was fitted up, and by favour of the Rev. Timothy Neve (subsequently Prebendary of Lincoln and of Peterborough and Archdeacon of Huntingdon), who hired that part, the Society met there at the usual times, until the number of members having increased they were obliged to find a larger room, and agreed to take one in the 'Markett-stead'.

It is evident that the Society was now in a most flourishing condition and had obtained a position seldom, if ever, equalled by any society in a provincial town. Extraneous assistance was, however needed, to sustain the interests of its members and maintain its prosperity. Papers were contributed, valuable books given, and interesting letters written by many who were not resident in the neighbourhood. These donations are still preserved with religious care. Some of the communications, e.g. from such men as Roger and Samuel Gale, Stukeley, the Earl of Oxford, Sir John Clarke, and others are of considerable interest. Four portfolios of drawings and engravings, several ancient manuscripts as well as books of reference, and many books printed in the fifteenth, sixteenth, and seventeenth centuries are still in the library. A commencement was also made towards forming a museum.

To the end of his life [in 1775] Maurice Johnson continued to be the mainstay of the Society. As long as he lived, the Society flourished. The greater part of the communications were made by him, or obtained through his activity. The minute books were chiefly his penmanship, and the beautiful illustrations therein mainly his handiwork. To the library he gave many of its most valuable books, and the museum owed much to his liberality. Even to the very last he showed his love for the Society , by providing in his will an endowment for the Chaplain of Wykeham, who was, previous to his appointment, to undertake the duties of librarian and take charge of its *supellex literaria*.

E. Mansel Sympson, M.A., M.D. (ed) Memorials of Old Lincolnshire *(1911)*, *pp. 319-329.*

6 · DRAMAS AND DISASTERS

The Removal of the Glass from Tattershall Church

In Tattershall church . . . there are more than 60 windows through which light streams
quite unhindered, for most of the lovely stained glass once here was taken to St Martin's Church, Stamford, in the eighteenth century. All that remains at Tattershall has been brought together in the great east window, where it looks like a pattern in a kaleidoscope.
Arthur Mee (ed), The King's England, Lincolnshire, *(1949), p 381.*

All previous accounts of the spoliation of the Chancel of Tattershall Church have given the date 1754. Mr. Wm. Banks, of Revesby, superintended the removal of the glass on behalf of Lord Exeter, to whom it had been given by Lord Fortescue, the proprietor of the chancel. The consideration of the gift was an agreement by Lord Exeter to re-glaze the windows with plain glass and repair all damage caused in removing the old glass. The Steward to Lord Fortescue, however, obtained a variation of this agreement by demanding the value in money of new glass and expense in replacing the old. The townspeople had evidently no hope of the Steward ever actually spending the money in the way it was intended to it should be, and their excitement caused a riot. I have in my possession, amongst a number of papers of the late Mr. Wm. Banks, some original and copy correspondence and memoranda relative to the removal of this glass, from which the letter below is taken. The letter is in Mr. Wm. Banks' handwriting, and though not signed or dated is endorsed 'Lord Exeter, copy of letter to him, 1757'.

From the endorsement on this letter, and also from the account of expenses incurred by him (also amongst his papers) it will be seen that the date of the removal of the glass was February 1757, and also that Lord Fortescue's Steward received on his behalf £24. 2s. 6d., the assessed cost of re-glazing and repairs. That the windows were for many years never re-glazed, and the chancel left to the mercy of the weather, and the consequences are of course well known.

'My Lord,

It gives me a good deal of concern that I am not able to acquaint your Lordship that the Tattershall windows are packt up and gone, which they might have been this day but for the following impediment, on Tuesday last, as the Glazier and his man had just finished their day's work they were assaulted in the Chancel by some low people of the Town, threatened wth Death if they returned to their work, abused and the Master struck. My servant Fowler who was in the Town made what enquiry he could into the cause of this riot which from what he heard imagine to be owing to this, that the People in the Town in general dislike the removal of the Glass because they believe that the Steward do's not intend to replace it wth new glass, and that they shall be left to say their prayers in a cold church at the hazard of their lives, moreover it has been intimated to him if it was proceeded in without new glass being put in as the old was taken out that the Boatmen on the River had engaged to assist the next riot & interrupt the work & he (Fowler) believes that without the assurance of replacing new Glass as we go on it could not be done without the hazard of the lives of those concerned in it. For these reasons I thought it best to send the workmen home till the return of the Steward who was then out on a journey not doubting but he would readily agree that I should proceed in that manner not having intimated before any intention of applying the value of the new glass to any other purpose but the use of the chancel but upon acquainting him wth the particulars he refuses that I should agree wth the People to put up the new glass till he has wrote to my Lord whom I believe he says he will never advise to repair the Chancel any more, so that the new glass if put in will be of no use but to please the People who have no concern therein, as the Chancel belongs intirely to my Lord.

I am sorry I should have advised yr Lordship to agree to that proposal of the Steward which has occasioned such delay. The Steward would have had us gone on but the Glazier had shewn so much fear on ye occasion yt I think it most prudent to stop till we be sure to proceed without Tumult or ye apprehension of it for in that case it is more yn probable if they were restrained from open riot they would do as much mischief by secret malice by perhaps breaking ye Glass or some such thing as by that. Therefore shall wait till I hear further from yr Lordship and am   My Lord &c.'

Lincolnshire Notes & Queries, *(1899), vol. 1, pp.1-3.*

The Louth Flood

The sad-faced lanky figure tossed two penny coins down on the bar counter with a 'Tek it; I'll starve' and returned to his wonted place on the settle clutching a short length of 'pigtail'. He slumped down and snorted 'Dang my blessed buttons if it ain't gone up another farthin'! 'ow much do they reckon a pipe o'baccy has to cost a man, eh? Answer me that, then!' He took out his clasp knife and sliced off a few rounds. He rolled them deliberately around in his horny palms, then packed and re-lit his clay.

He glanced sideways at the portly figure and held out the remaining finger of tobacco. The other was staring thoughtfully into the fire and shook his head slowly without once bothering to look up. How much does a pipe o'baccy have to cost a man? Well, more than this particular man dreamed possible and perhaps more than you will ever know, mused Abe. The words swam before him with prophetic poignancy. Tonight of all nights; Saturday, 29th May, 1934 . . . fourteen years ago to the very day!

It had all seemed to stem from those terrible nightmares he'd had, night after night, and always shot through with some impending doom. It always began with a shopping expedition to Louth and his becoming separated from Amelia. Then suddenly, this terrible wall of water roaring down on them, snatching everyone and everything into its seething maelstrom. Bursting lungs, knifed through with white hot fire and weird green lights playing behind his eyes: a death's head, bobbing and dipping, grinning obscenely, it grew into a woman's white, lifeless face that sped by . . . elusive and tantalisingly familiar. He awoke, as always, soaked in perspiration and shouting grotesque, meaningless sounds. These repeated outbursts upset Amelia dreadfully, the more so because he could not bear to talk to her about them. Then, as suddenly as they had begun, they stopped.

It was 29th May 1920 and they had been spending a few days at Rose Lea with 'Grumps'. An outing to Louth had been decided upon to heighten their holiday enjoyment and the day dawned dull but with a hint of rain. 'Grumps' found he needed an ounce of his favourite tobacco. Amelia announced she would be perfectly satisfied just to stroll around the Market Place and market hall . . . but nevertheless she had her heart set upon a length of wide scarlet ribbon with which to trim her old hat. He himself was thinking more of boiled sweets, acid drops or pear drops, or perhaps even some of those pink and white fishes at a penny three farthings a quarter.

They eventually caught the one forty-eight from South Willingham station and arrived at Louth at quarter past two. Amelia was pleased that she had relented and accepted the loan of 'Grumps' funny, old-fashioned umbrella for the sky was even more overcast. Shopping completed they rounded off their expedition with a visit to a café for a pot of tea and a cake each. All very exciting and extravagant!

By now it was past five o'clock and time to be catching the five-forty back to South Willingham with their precious purchases. She patted her coat pocket in which reposed her red ribbon and Abe was carrying 'Grumps' mixed shag; all very wicked and self-indulgent. The weather wasn't so nice now. The air seemed abnormally still and it was raining quite heavily when they emerged from the café. Thunder was growling menacingly in Hubbard's Hill Valley and they huddled together beneath 'Grumps' huge umbrella and made a run for it to the shelter of the railway station. The rain gradually increased in intensity as they went until it was falling in torrents.

'In here, Amelia!' shouted Abe ducking into a nearby doorway. 'Us'll get soaked, else!' Moments later, no Amelia appearing, he peered out at a grey, hissing curtain of water. He felt a strange wind on his face, and a roaring noise in his ears. He turned to face the sound and what he saw froze the very marrow in his bones. A solid wall of water, man high, was careering along towards him with the speed of an express train. 'Dear God,' he whispered, in disbelief. 'Whatever is it?' The watery avalanche struck him with unimaginable ferocity, snatching him from the doorway and flinging him amongst a jumble of surface flotsam . . . smashed barrels, dead animals, ladders, broken sheds, shattered trees . . . all swirling about him as if bent upon his immediate destruction.

Occasionally, he fancied he heard voices screaming, calling, pleading. He wondered what was happening to Amelia. It was as if it had all happened before, somewhere. It was something he was living out again, that's all. Perhaps he was dead. He toyed with the thought for a while, then he was falling . . . falling. A battering ram of water had punched a gap three houses wide and had fanned out into the open space beyond. He rushed headlong through, striking something resistant. He clutched with unknowing desperation and found himself wedged. They found him there a few hours later.

Perhaps the worst part of all was when he was called upon to identify Amelia's body. It had not been easy. They had finally located her below an accumulated excretion of slime, bricks and sundry debris. The cadaver, grotesque from its violent battering, moved him hardly at all. He found it utterly impossible to relate it to Amelia. It was merely a . . . a thing! It was only when they showed him an item they had removed from the coat pocket that it came home to him. It was a grubby length of what had once been a pretty red ribbon. He broke down and wept uncontrollably.

It was much later that he was able to set his own loss against the overall picture. Twenty-three others had perished that awful day. The most tragic that he remembered concerned a mother and her young family who were trapped by water that rose so quickly they were unable to reach safety upstairs. She lifted three of her children onto the kitchen dresser, finally climbing up herself with a year-old baby in her arms. As the water level continued to rise, she clutched with one hand to a ceiling bacon hook. The children hung onto her skirts for as long as they were able but gradually, one by one, they lost their hold and sank back into the water to be drowned before their agonised mother's eyes. The dresser was now floating and the gaslight had been extinguished by the water. Mother and one surviving child were rescued later that evening.

Over a period of time, all manner of stories of courage and of reasons for the flood emerged. It transpired that something like nine million tons of water had descended on Louth that awful day, by way of Hubbard's Hills and the river Lud. Debris of all kinds had blocked culverts and bridges thereby effectively damming the water. It was said that at Little Welton, pressure overcame the barrier and the collected water descended into the town. The gentle Lud was now 200 yards wide and it took to the streets, sweeping all before it. It was reputed to have risen sixteen feet in fifteen minutes.

The sudden rise in the flood water was due largely to its flow being impeded by houses at right angles to the ends of the streets. Their downfall was the salvation of many others, for water backed up to such good effect that it swept three houses on the east side of Ramsgate away with hardly one brick remaining upon another . . . thereby lowering the flood level almost as quickly as it had risen.

When the final balance sheet had been drawn it emerged that, on the debit side, 24 people had lost their lives, three houses had been swept away, 43 had to be demolished and 173 were rendered partially uninhabitable. There had been a great loss of livestock and crops. On the credit side, it had been Saturday and children were out of school. Most grown-ups had been indoors at the time and the streets were almost clear by nine-thirty pm. A Flood Relief Fund was initiated by the Mayor of Louth and the response was both immediate and generous, £90,000 being subscribed.

When old 'Grumps' had died, some five years later, Abe had discovered in a secret drawer of the bureau a grubby little packet of what looked like tobacco. It smelled strongly of earth mould.

As Abe started reflectively into the log fire of the Snug he grew aware of someone poking him in the ribs. 'Wek up, old un! I were just sayin' . . . what a shockin' price to pay for a spot o'baccy!'

Roy Fisk, Lincolnshire Medley, pp. 95-98.

High Tides

The low lying coastal lands have always been prone to flooding but over the centuries storms have also caused havoc further inland. There were disastrous floods in the Marsh in 1253 and 1315, great flooding at Boston in 1285 and in 'Holland' in 1467, and many more have been recorded over the last five hundred years. But it was the violent storms of 1571 that caused so much devastation. The combination of rain, wind and a high tide did a huge amount of damage. Sixty vessels were wrecked along the coast and thousands of cattle and sheep were drowned in the Marsh. The village of Mumby Chapel all but disappeared with only three cottages and the church steeple remaining. It was not just the Marsh and the coast that suffered. Inland, as far as the Soke of Peterborough, the sudden and violent rise of the flood demolished three arches of the bridge that crossed the River Nene at Wansford. It was the same storm that reached half way up Bourne church tower.

It was this terrible flooding that captured the imagination of Boston poet Jean Ingelow, who wrote a long, incredibly moving poem called The High Tide on the Coast of Lincolnshire (1571) *where she tells of the Boston bells ringing out the alarm with 'The Brides of Enderby'. I've included the central section, in which the narrator's son brings news of the storm and of the flood waters surging up river. 'Lindis' is the old name for North Lincolnshire.*

'The olde sea wall (he cried) is downe,
   The rising tide comes on apace,
The boats adrift in yonder towne
   Go sailing uppe the market place.'
He shook as one that looks on death:
'God save you mother!' straight he saith;
'Where is my wife, Elizabeth?'

'Good sonne, where Lindis winds away,
   With her two bairns I marked her long;
And ere yon bells beganne to play
   Afar I heard her milking song.'
He looked across the grassy lea.

To right, to left, 'Ho, Enderby!'
They rang 'The Brides of Enderby'!

With that he cried and beat his breast;
    For lo! Along the river's bed
A mighty eygre reared his crest,
    And uppe the Lindis raging sped.
It swept with thundrous noises loud;
Shaped like a curling, snow-white cloud,
Or like a demon in a shroud.

And rearing Lindis backward pressed
    Shook all her trembling bankes amaine;
Then madly at the eygre's breast
    Flung uppe her weltering walls again.
Then banks came down with ruin and rout –
The beaten foam flew round about –
Then all the mighty floods were out.

So farre, so fast the eygre drave,
    The heart had hardly time to beat,
Before a shallow seething wave
    Sobbed in the grasses at oure feet:
The feet had hardly time to flee
Before it brake against the knee,
And all the world was in the sea.

Upon the roofe we sate that night,
    The noise of bells went sweeping by:
I marked a lofty beacon light
    Stream from the church tower, red and high –
A lurid mark and dread to see;
And awesome bells they were to mee,
That in the dark rang 'Enderby'.

They rang the sailor lads to guide
    From roofe to roofe who fearless rowed;
And I – my sonne was at my side,

And yet the ruddy beacon glowed;
And yet he moaned beneath his breath,
'O come in life, or come in death!
O lost! My love, Elizabeth.'

The Poetry Society, A Book of Lincolnshire Verse, *(1930), p. 41*

7 · WORTHIES

The Story of John Smith

Is there something about Lincolnshire that produces people who make their mark in history? Even if they were not born in Lincolnshire, many people of repute (and disrepute) have spent a considerable time here. Alfred, Lord Tennyson, poet laureate, Margaret Thatcher, prime minister, John Wesley, the founder of Methodism, Dame Sybil Thorndyke, actress, William Booth, founder of the Salvation Army, Chad Varah, founder of the Samaritans, Geoff Capes, the world's strongest man in his heyday, and Joseph Banks, botanist, were all born in the county. So were Group Captain Leonard Cheshire, Guy Gibson, Henry IV, Isaac Newton, William Cecil, Gilbert of Sempringham and John Smith. John Smith? This is how Adrian Gray tells his story.

John Smith was born in Willoughby, a village in the eastern part of Lincolnshire, in 1579. Though he was blessed with perhaps the most ordinary of names, he proved to be the most extraordinary person whose fame is now firmly established on both sides of the Atlantic Ocean.

As a young boy, Smith was sent to school in the market town of Alford and there he heard of the great deeds of Francis Drake – pirate, explorer and national hero. At the age of 13 Smith decided to follow in Drake's footsteps and immediately began to prepare to run away to sea. He sold all his school books to finance the venture, but was stopped by his father who had discovered his plan.

Smith left school and was sent to Louth for two years and then went to King's Lynn as an apprentice to a merchant. However, Smith was not cut out for a career behind a desk and, when his father died, he left England and joined the army in the Netherlands. Smith enjoyed a successful career in the Netherlands and France, reports of his deeds being heard even in little Willoughby. He then took passage in a fishing boat in order to reach Scotland but was nearly drowned when it was wrecked off the coast of Northumberland. He decided to return to his home village for a while but he had become famous and found the attention he received while living at home to be most irritating. He left the house and moved out into the woods, building himself a shelter in which he could sit and study the works of Machiavelli. Smith clearly did not intend staying in Lincolnshire for he borrowed a riding master from the Earl of Lincoln so that he could improve his skills.

He then returned to the Netherlands and there decided to enlist in the struggle against the Turks in south-east Europe. He travelled to France, from where he hoped to get a ship going east, but was tricked by a group of Frenchmen and lost all his possessions. Things got worse when Smith boarded a ship going from Marseilles to Rome for it was discovered that he was a Protestant and the Catholics aboard threw him over the side.

Fortunately, Smith was a good swimmer and survived this latest upset in his career. He managed to board another ship going to Tunisia, from there progressing to Egypt and Corfu. While his ship was passing through the Adriatic Sea it encountered a merchant ship from Venice, and attacked. Smith took part in this act of piracy and a cargo of silk was captured. His share was enough to make him a rich man again.

Eventually Smith managed to join the Imperial Army at Graz, now in Austria, for its struggle against the Muslim Turks. He was soon in the thick of things, showing great skill in the battle of Limbach where Smith, confused the Turks with his diversionary tactics. The Imperial Army then moved on to besiege a Turkish garrison, during which

Smith devised a novel weapon: he filled old pitchers with gunpowder, pieces of bullets and other metal, then stuck a piece of inflammable cloth in the top before catapulting them over the walls at night.

In Romania, where Muslims and Christians had been fighting for centuries, Smith accepted a duel to the death against a Turkish champion. Smith duly won, cut off the head of the defeated man, and presented it to his general. On the next two days he fought equally successful battles against other Turkish challengers, each time repeating the ceremony of the head. Following these battles, Smith carried a shield emblazoned with three Turkish head emblems.

In 1602, Smith was captured by the Turks and forced into slavery. However his Turkish master beat him one day and this was more than Smith could endure; he turned on the man, killed him, and escaped in his clothes, eventually reaching the safety of Russia.

He returned to England, but was lured by the promise of excitement in the new American colonies. He decided to join an expedition to Virginia, but on the voyage across the Atlantic he was nearly executed for mutiny. In 1607 he landed at Chesapeake Bay and helped set up Jamestown.

Smith spent a lot of his time dealing with the Indians and became an expert in their ways. Because of his trading links with them, the settlers were able to avoid the worst effects of a famine. But Smith then joined an expedition to find Chief Powhatan which turned into a disaster – all the settlers except Smith were killed and he was eventually surrounded by 200 Indians. Rather than kill him, however, they took him to their chief.

Smith impressed the chief by showing him a compass and talking about the movement of the stars. He narrowly escaped execution once more, but was kept a prisoner though he was well fed – because of this Smith feared he might become a cannibal's dinner. He managed to trick the Indians into taking a message to Jamestown and he received a letter in reply; using the letter Smith was able to convince them that paper could speak!

None of this could save him from being taken to Powhatan and when Smith's head was laid on an altar he felt certain that his end had at last arrived. Just at the last second, though, a little Indian maid pleaded for his life. She was Pocahontas, Powhatan's daughter. The chief listened to his daughter and agreed to ransom Smith for a grindstone and two guns – thus he escaped once more!

His next escape from death came when he was leading an expedition to explore the river Potomac. While fishing, Smith received a poisonous sting from a sting-ray and nearly died.

In 1608 Smith was elected President of the Council of Virginia and made another bargaining trip to Powhatan. Once more he ran into trouble and once more he was saved by Pocahontas' intervention. She eventually married another Englishman, John Rolfe, and died at Gravesend in Kent in 1617.

Smith returned to England in 1609, disabled by burns sustained in an accident with gunpowder, He returned to America in 1614 and led an expedition to Maine where English settlers were fighting the French. However, Smith was captured by the enemy in 1615 and taken prisoner on board a ship; he escaped by stealing the ship's boat following which the ship itself promptly sank.

Smith spent his last years more sedately, writing about New England. He died at the age of 51, having cheated death on many previous occasions.

Adrian Gray, Tales of Old Lincolnshire, *(1990), pp.35 – 38.*

The Kings' Champions

John Ketteringham tells the story of the Kings' Champions, the Dymokes of Scrivelsby. The original role of the King's Champion was to challenge all-comers to the throne on behalf of the monarch. The post was hereditar, but by 1820, the date of George IV's Coronation and the last time a Dymoke bore arms on behalf of the crown, it had become ceremonial.

Scrivelsby Court is situated on the road from Horncastle to Revesby. The gateway is surmounted by a crowned lion, thus marking it as the home of the Sovereign's Champion. The way in which the Lord of the Manor of Scrivelsby acquired the right to this title is very interesting.

Near Falaise, where William the Conqueror was born, is a village called Fontenay-le-Marmion. The Marmion family acted as Champions to the Dukes of Normandy and when William invaded England it was Robert Marmion who accompanied him as Champion.

After the Conquest, Marmion was granted land which included Tamworth Castle, but the Manor of Scrivelsby was particularly assigned to him as Champion to the Sovereign. Though the descendants of Sir Robert continued to be recognised as King's Champions, there is no record before the reign of Richard II of their being called upon to carry out any special duties at a coronation. In 1292 Sir Philip, one of the last and greatest of the Marmion family, died without a male heir and in 1350 his grand-daughter married Sir John Dymock who claimed the Championship. This was upheld and he carried out the duty at Richard II's coronation.

At the twenty-five coronations since, it has always been a Dymoke of Scrivelsby who has officiated and only at the coronations of William IV and Queen Victoria was this part of the ceremony omitted. At the coronation of Richard II in 1377 the procedure for all succeeding coronations was laid down.

During the banquet in Westminster Hall the Champion enters clad in full armour, mounted on a white horse. The armour is selected from the Sovereign's Armoury and the horse from the Sovereign's Stables. The Champion is preceded by two knights who carry his spear and shield, with the Earl Marshall riding on his left and the Lord High Constable on his right. Three times York Herald challenges to mortal combat any person who denies the Sovereign to be the rightful heir to the crown of England. Three times York Herald throws down his gauntlet which after a while is delivered to him again. The third time the Challenge is made from the top steps in the middle of the hall before the Sovereign, who is then presented with a gold cup full of wine. The Sovereign then drinks to the Champion, after which the cup is delivered to him and after three bows he drinks the wine, shouting 'Long live their Majesties' and then withdraws backwards from their presence. The cup then becomes the property of the Champion.

It is said that at the coronation of James II in 1685, a woman stepped forward and took up the gauntlet, leaving a paper to say that a Champion of rank and birth would dispute the King's claim to the throne. However, no more was heard of this and there is some doubt of the truth of the story.

During the Wars of the Roses, Sir Thomas Dymoke supported the Lancastrians and was beheaded by the order of Edward IV. The King tried to atone for this act by conferring honours on the heir, Sir

Robert. During the Civil War, the King's Champion, Charles Dymoke, supported the royal cause, even leaving £2,000 on his death to help the King. His successor, Edward Dymoke, was accused by Parliamentarians of bearing the 'lewd and malicious' title of King's Champion and was fined £7,000.

The last coronation at which the elaborate ceremonial was enacted was that of George IV and since that of Edward VII, the task of the Sovereign's Champion has been to carry the Standard of England.

John Ketteringham, Lincolnshire People, *(1995), pp. 33-34.*

William Stukeley

The antiquarian and pioneering archaeologist William Stukeley was born in Holbeach.

Dr. Wm. Stukeley, 1687-1765, was a famous Lincolnshire antiquarian. He practised medicine, first at Boston and then at Grantham from 1710 to 1726. He was made an FRS in 1717, and in that or the following year he helped to establish the Society of Antiquaries in London, and was for the first nine years secretary to that Society. In 1719 he became an MD of Cambridge and was made a member of the Spalding Gentlemen's Society in 1722. In 1727 he took Holy Orders and from 1730 to 1748 officiated as Vicar of All Saints at Stamford where he founded the shortlived Brazenose Society. He was a great friend of Sir Isaac Newton and kept up his interest in scientific matters to the end, inasmuch as he put off his service on one occasion in order that his congregation might watch an eclipse of the sun. Whilst still Vicar of Stamford he was made Rector of Somerby near Grantham, 1739-1747, but he retired from both livings in 1748, and spent the rest of his life in London, where at the age of 75 he preached his first sermon in spectacles, taking as his text 'now we see through a glass darkly.'

W. F. Rawnsley, Highways and Byways of Lincolnshire, *(1914), p. 500.*

Alfred, Lord Tennyson

Alfred, Lord Tennyson was born at Somersby where his father was rector, in 1809. He was one of twelve children and a great reader as well as a prolific poet. The family moved away from Lincolnshire in 1837 but Alfred left behind a little local legacy of poetry. The Elizabethan walled garden at Harrington Hall is said to be his inspiration for 'Maud' and the stream that ran through the village is immortalised in 'The Brook'. His sadness in leaving Somersby is captured in these words.

Unwatched, the garden bough shall sway,
   The tender blossom flutter down,
   Unloved that beech will gather brown,
This maple burn itself away;

Unloved, the sun-flower, shining fair,
   Ray round with flames her disk of seed,
   And many a rose-carnation feed
With summer spice the humming air;

Unloved, by many a sandy bar,
   The brook shall babble down the plain,
   At noon or when the lesser wain
Is twisting round the polar star;

Uncared for, gird the windy grove,
   And floods the haunts of hern and crake;
   Or into silver arrows break
The sailing moon is creek and cove

Till from the garden and the wild
   A fresh association blow,
   And year by year the landscape grow
Familiar to the stranger's child;

As year by year the labourer tills
   His wonted glebe, or lops the glades;
   And year by year our memory fades
From all the circle of the hills.

Alfred, Lord Tennyson, from In Memoriam

Daniel Lambert

Daniel Lambert was once the fattest man in England. At his death he weighed 52 stones 11 pounds, his waist measuring 9ft 4ins and his calf 3ft 1in. Born in Leicester in 1770 he died in Stamford, Lincolnshire in 1809. His stick and chair are underneath his portrait in the hall of The George Hotel in the town.

When Daniel was fourteen he was sent as an apprentice to Mr Benjamin Patrick of Messrs Taylor & Co, engravers and die sinkers in Birmingham. But the business was destroyed in the riots of 1791 and shortly after he succeeded his father as keeper of the prison (in Leicester).

At the same time he began to increase in weight and by 1793 he turned the scale at 32 stone. Even so, he could walk from Woolwich to the metropolis with little apparent fatigue. He was a keen huntsman, bred terriers, and at the age of 28 could lift five-hundredweight with ease.

Once, when his dog attacked a performing bear and was likely to be killed, he seized a pole from the trainer to strike the bear, and slipped under the beast. The bystanders were horrified, but he struck the bear such a blow on the skull with his hand that she 'declined the contest, and yelling, fled'.

Lambert fulfilled his office as gaoler with firmness and ability, and 'never forebore to make the greatest exertions to assist them (the prisoners) at the time of their trials. Few left the prison without testifying their gratitude, and tears often spoke the sincerity of the feelings they expressed'. The magistrates, when the prison closed in 1805, granted him an annuity of £50 for life, 'a declaration of the universal satisfaction which he had given in the discharge of the duties of his office'.

He then decided, albeit with reluctance, to exhibit himself in London, and took an apartment at 53 Piccadilly, whither he travelled in a specially constructed coach (April 4 1806). His ready wit and courteous bearing made his lodging a rendezvous of society, and, in spite of the admission fee of 1/-, turned what might have been a sordid peep-show into a social occasion. One visitor, who had obtained a personal interview on the pretext of asking advice about a horse, received the deserved reply 'She was got by Impertinence out of

Curiosity'.

Fourteen people came from Guernsey specially to see him as did the Polish dwarf Count Borulawski. Even Quakers, we are told, removed their hats in his presence. A woman once asked him the cost of his coat. He replied 'If you think proper to make me a present of a new coat, you will then know exactly what it costs.'

After five months in London he returned to Leicester and lived in seclusion there. In March 1807 he again visited London, and later travelled to various other towns, till in 1809 he went through Huntingdon to Stamford to the races. Here he lodged at the Waggon and Horses Inn in St Martins, and died suddenly at 9.00am on Wednesday 21st June. His body was extracted from the ground floor room in which he perforce had been accommodated, by demolishing a wall, and was placed in a coffin built on wheels and containing 112 superficial feet of elm. Upwards of twenty men lowered it down a ramp into his grave in St Martin's Churchyard.

So died Daniel Lambert. Since he was a teetotaller 'but convivial', and never ate more than one dish at meals, his corpulence must have been due to disease. It did not cause him any pain. He never snored, could awake within five minutes of any time he pleased, rarely retired before 1 am, and never slept for more than 8 hours, always with the window open. He never caught a cold, even when he slept in saturated clothing. He could sing a strong tenor, and never married, though he was 'very partial to the female sex'.

David T-D Clarke,, Daniel Lambert, (1973 third edition), pp. 1-5.

Old Families

Lincolnshire names continue to pepper the county. The really old family names include Darcy, Kyme, de Roos, Trehampton and the Lincolnshire Neviles. The Watertons, the Thorolds, the Heneages, the Massingberds, the Tyrwhits and the Dymokes all held lands in the county and were as well known as the Ayscoughs, the Copledikes, the Asfordbys, the Custs and the Monsons. Canon Maddison, at the end of a paper about Lincolnshire families, gives his opinion on the unauthorised use of a coat-of-arms and the extinction of many families.

To give an exhaustive list of all the old families in this county, and to trace their fortunes, would be absolutely beyond the scope of this paper. All that can be done is to give a sketch of those families which still survive in the male line after the vicissitudes of several centuries. They are not numerous. Others, such as the Turnors of Stoke Rochford, the Sibthorps of Canwick, the Nelthorpes of Scawby, came in with the Commonwealth. A multitude sprang up in the eighteenth century, and have been largely recruited in the nineteenth. It may be questioned whether Gervase Holles would recognise many of the names which would meet his eye in the list of magistrates. It is still more open to question whether a herald of 1562 would not 'respite for further proof' a good deal of modern heraldry. To bear another man's coat-of-arms because you happen to be of the same name would scarcely pass muster with a sixteenth century herald, but it is an innocent appropriation by no means uncommon at the present day.

I may add a word on the subject of extinction of old mediaeval families. Are they really extinct? Names are found among the peasantry which at first sight suggest a negative to that question, but I have never yet met with an authentic instance of such descent. The one that occurs to me as most probable is that of the Bushey family. Families of that name were at Leverton, Leake and Friskney three hundred years ago, and doubtless there are descendents in the male line. The name Bushey is identical with Bussy; in fact, the pronunciation of the name at the time of the execution of Sir John Bussy, Richard II's favourite, in 1398, was undoubtedly Bushey, as the punning rhymes made upon it by writers of that day testify, e.g. –

> Ther is a *busch* that is forgrow,
> Crop hit welle and hold it lowe,
> Or elles it wolle be wilde.

There is therefore some ground for supposing that these yeoman families may have descended from cadet branches of this race which held so high a position in the fourteenth and fifteenth centuries, though positive proof is wanting.

It would be extremely interesting to trace, if possible, the descent of such families, but the difficulties are very great. The absence of wills of yeoman families prior to the fifteenth century is one great obstacle; the dearth of documents in that century is another.

E Mansel Sympson, Memorials of Old Lincolnshire, (1911), pp. 317-318.

Gunby Hall

After being invalided out of the army in 1941, James Lees-Milne rejoined the then small staff of the National Trust. Over the next two years he visited numerous stately homes and historic houses whose owners, for various reasons, wished to hand them over to the Trust. These two excerpts from his diary for 1943 recount a visit to Gunby Hall, then the home of Field Marshall Sir A. Montgomery-Massingberd.

Wednesday, 10th November
I left for Lincolnshire, arriving at Gunby Hall at 7.45 in time for dinner. The old Field-Marshall [Montgomery-Massingberd] in his dark velvet jacket and expanse of dazzling evening shirt looked inconceivably white in the face. At first glance he appears the epitome of blimpishness. In fact he is benign, simple-hearted and understanding. Lady Massingberd is vivacious, a little bit arch, and very godly and kind, not to say motherly. After dinner we talked exclusively of Gunby's future. They both adore this place.

Thursday 11th November
Today was bright, sunny and very cold. Yet after breakfast the field-marshal took me walking to the chalk pits and the northern part of the estate. He moves very slowly, muffled up in a raincoat, and voluminous scarf, and wearing enormous gumboots. Every six yards he stands stock still to emphasise a point, while I freeze. He seems impervious to the cold. Whenever he meets someone he stops again. He is charming to, almost humble with his servants and tenants, and especially the ordinary soldiers. After luncheon we walked over the other part of the estate, across the railway line to Bratoft, where we looked at the square moat of the Massingberds' old castle, destroyed when Gunby was built. Nothing else remains...A huge steel structure like the Eiffel Tower with a beacon on the top has been erected on the tennis court, close to the house, as a guide to pilots and a safeguard of the house. I am overjoyed that the Trust has been largely instrumental in preventing this dear old place from being razed to the ground in order to extend the runway.

James Lees-Milne, Ancestral Voices, *(1975), pp. 267-268.*

Boston Notables

Boston's contribution to the world has been exceptional by any standard. Apart from its associations with the early Pilgrim Fathers (who were imprisoned there in 1607 after they had been betrayed by the Dutch captain on whose ship they were sailing to escape religious persecution), the town was also the birthplace in 1516 of John Foxe, the author of what is now commonly known as Foxe's Book of Martyrs.

Boston can also claim John Taverner (1490-1545), the great Tudor composer of madrigals, and the poet, Jean Inglelow, (1820-97), whose ballad 'High Tide on the Coast of Lincolnshire, 1571', still appears regularly in anthologies of English verse. The town's tradition of producing such creative minds continued with the birth in 1926 of one of today's outstanding poets, Elizabeth Jennings.

There are earlier literary associations with John Conington (1825-69), who, in his short life, translated much of Virgil. Aeschylus and Horace and also with Herbert Ingram, the founding editor of the still popular journal *The Illustrated London News*. Ingram, remembered in the town by his statue near the church, was drowned in 1860 while on tour in America.

Edward Storey, Spirit of the Fens, *(1985), p. 161.*

8 · FOLKLORE

There are rich pickings to be found in the folk tales of the county. Here are a few; some may well be found in other parts of Britain, others are strictly Lincolnshire. Some should definitely be taken with a pinch of salt.

The Winceby stone

There was the large stone in Winceby field, where soldiers had sharpened their swords before the battle. This was a stone of fearful interest, for much treasure was supposed to have been buried under it. Numerous attempts have been made to get at this treasure, but they were always defeated by some accident or piece of bad luck. On the last occasion, by 'yokking' several horses to chains fastened round the stone, they nearly succeeded in pulling it over, when, in his excitement, one of the men uttered an oath, and the devil instantly appeared, and stamped on it with his foot. 'Tha cheans all brok, tha osses fell, an' tha stoan went back t' its owd place solidder nur ivver; an' if ya doan't believe ya ma goa an' look fur yer sen, an' ya'll see tha divvill's fut mark like three kraws' claws, a-top o' tha stoan.' It was firmly believed the lane was haunted, and that loud groans were often heard there.
Lincolnshire Notes & Queries, *(1899) vol. ix, p.446.*

June Water

There is a Lincolnshire saying that whenever water is drawn from a well a little should be thrown back into it. And only a few years ago a woman, who was born about 1812 in a parish lying within three or four miles of the southern bank of the Humber, presented one of her carefully hoarded bottles of 'June-water' to a friend, with the assurance that it was a household remedy of the greatest value for bad eyes and other ailments, and that it had been caught as it had fallen direct from the clouds – 'None of your eaves' drip nor tree-drip, but straight from the sky.' In Lancashire such 'June-water' has also an established reputation; but in the wapentake of Walshcroft, in Lincolnshire, another version of the belief has currency. It is there thought by some people that 'July-water' possesses health-restoring qualities.

Lincolnshire Notes & Queries, *(1899) vol. ix, p.446.*

Bourne Meadow-letting

A singular custom has been practised here every year ever since the year 1770, when Richard Clay left a piece of land, the rent of which was to be laid out in bread for the inhabitants. The meadow is let from year to year in a curious manner: an auctioneer attends and starts a number of boys running at a fixed distance. As soon as they have set off, he asks the people who wish to rent the field to commence bidding. As bids can only be made while the boys are running, the bidding becomes very keen. At last, as the boys return, down goes the hammer, and the last bidder is declared the lessee.

Kelly's Directory of Lincolnshire, *(1930)*

Riding the Stang

In the north of Lincolnshire the custom of riding the stang, in the case of a man and wife quarrelling, is not uncommon. The farming lads assemble, one is placed on a pole astride, and they go with tongs and kettles to the door of the unlucky couple and recite some verses, of which one will suffice as a specimen:

He banged her wi' stick,

He banged her wi' steean,

He teeak op his neeaf,

    An' he knocked her doon.

    With a ran, tan, tan, etc.

The word 'neaf, for fist, is pure Danish, and the stang is probably a relic of the nid-stang, or pole of infamy, of the Scandinavians. 'With a ran, tan, tan' is a jingle...applied to delinquents who had behaved badly to their wives. The sound is essentially connected with a noise – raising a din, attracting attention, before, as it were, reading the indictment.

Lincolnshire Notes & Queries, *(1899) vol iv, p.189.*

The Devil, the Imp and the East Wind

Lincoln Cathedral is said to be one of the finest mediaeval buildings in Europe. Upon completion the monks believed the devil could not resist being malicious to such a wonderful place of worship and that he viewed it with a sour and evil expression, hence the adage, 'He looks as the devil over Lincoln.'

Its exposed situation and the rather dissolute life of some of the clergy centuries ago gave rise to the following legend.

The devil became friendly with the wind and they went together to the cathedral. Satan told his companion to wait outside whilst he went in to have a chat with the dean and chapter. The wind agreed and has been waiting ever since and one presumes the devil has found a lot to discuss with the dean and chapter! His intimate alliance with the wind suggests that he has taken the place of Odin, a heathen 'Prince of the Powers of the Air,' greatly honoured by the Vikings who settled in eastern England.

The famous Lincolnshire Imp is one of many devils to be found in the cathedral and sits at the cleft of a pillar adjacent to the east window, above the Angel Choir. The following is a popular tales concerning its presence.

Once a strong wind brought two imps to see the newly built cathedral at Lincoln. The first, who was curious to see what such a holy place had to offer, slipped in unnoticed and was so amazed at what it saw and heard, that its heart turned to stone and the creature became rooted to the ground. The other imp went looking for its brother and unwittingly alighted on the shoulders of a witch, who flew round the ceiling and deposited the imp, which she turned to stone, on its now well known perch. The wind, which always seems to be blowing, still haunts the Minster precincts waiting for the return of the imps.

Polly Howat, Ghosts & Legends of Lincolnshire & the Fen Country, *(1992), pp. 51-52.*

Hassock-throwing

The following is a most extraordinary story of the supposed happenings at wedding ceremonies.

There used to prevail in Donington a custom for the old women in the parish to assemble in the nave of the church on the occasion of a wedding and as the bridal party moved up the chancel, to pelt them with hassocks. Once within the chancel screen the bride and her friends were safe, but the old women still kept up the game among themselves by hurling the hassocks at one another. It would seem that the clergy at Donington-on-Bain did not mind this remarkable behaviour in church until about the year 1780 when Mr Veners, a relative of Lord Monson, became rector. He was probably not aware of the singular 'Old English' game of the old ladies, but on the occasion of the first wedding he celebrated, they were at their posts in church, shouldering their arms – the hassocks as usual. The bridal party was standing just outside the chancel gates. The rector, himself, in his surplice was passing under the screen, when a hassock missed its aim and struck Mr Veners on the back. He looked round, very frightened and feeling scandalised when he saw the hassocks flying fast and furiously, as his elderly female parishioners entered into the spirit of the game, and kept it up with ardour, unabated by the chill of age. The custom then rightly came to an end.

The Louth and District Directory and Recorder, *(1927).*

Little St Hugh

Half way down the south choir aisle of Lincoln Cathedral is the remains of the shrine of Little St Hugh, said to have been murdered in 1255. At that time, and in common with many other cities, Lincoln had a larger and prosperous Jewish community which was blamed for the boy's death and subsequent communal revenge.

The eight years old boy was alleged to have been murdered by a Jew named Copin, who lived at the foot of Steep Hill, Lincoln, whose daughter enticed the little boy over the wall and into their garden with the promise of an apple. He was seized and brought before a mock jury, then later tortured, crucified and murdered. When the boy failed to return home his mother sent out a search party which discovered his body at the bottom of a well belonging to a Jew's house.

The King's Justiciary, John de Lexington, was in Lincoln at the time of the crime and ordered Copin to be seized and questioned. On pardon for his life he is said to have confessed to the murder and explained that the child had been put to death in front of a great many Jews who had gathered at Lincoln for the occasion, to avenge the crucifixion of Christ. One of their number elected to represent Pilate had ordered the punishment and eventual execution of the boy. The prisoner also admitted that it was the custom of the Jews to sacrifice a Christian child in this fashion every year, which was a popular story of the time.

Polly Howat, Ghosts & Legends of Lincolnshire & the Fen Country, (1992), pp52-53.

Tuttings

The tuttings, for their singularity, for their singularity deserve a short notice, especially as the custom of holding them is now fast descending into the vale of oblivion, and as it may enable our readers to form some idea of the manner in which the common people of Lincoln used formerly to divert themselves. The following is the manner in which these meetings were generally held: a landlady who wished to have a tutting gave notice of her intentions to all her female acquaintances, whether married or single. On the day and the hour specified, the visitors assembled, and were regaled with tea (so far all well); but on the removal of that, the table was replenished with a bowl and glasses, and exhilarated with potent punch, when each guest became a new creature. About this time the husbands, or cecisbeos, arrived, paid their half guineas each for the treatment of themselves and partners, joined the revelry and partook of the amusements proposed by their *cheres amies*. Each female then, anxious to please her partner for the evening, displayed every captivating charm, either in the enlivening catch, the witty *double entendre*, the dance, or beating of the tambourine, till every decency was often forgotten and the restraints of modesty abandoned. This custom, which was confined solely to the lower ranks, is now, very properly, almost abolished.

From *The History of Lincoln*, printed by A Stark, 1810, pp. 273-4.
Ethel H Rudkin, Lincolnshire Folklore, *(1936), p. 55*.

Why Lincolnshire Yellow-belly?

People born in Lincolnshire are known as yellow-bellies. Why is unclear. Are they named for the frog with the yellow front, the eels found in the dykes or the yellow stomachs of the sheep feeding on the mustard crops? My favourite explanation suggests that when the farmers were harvesting mustard and the weather was hot, they removed their shirts. At the end of the day their torsos were stained with the yellow powder. Roy Fisk teases us about the meaning.

If the source of the phrase Lincolnshire Yellow-belly were to be established once and for all, with no questionable doubt, would not the subject lose its interest? It is, by its very nature, one that latches on to the imagination and offers plenty of scope for invention. Perhaps this is why there are so many different theories. The more 'origins' that appear, the greater our perplexity and fascination. It is a self-generating thing.

The phrase has to have its roots in the past, doesn't it? 'Belly' is rather too coarse a word for our sophisticated palate (or rather was, until the recent explosion of permissive talk and behaviour), and

'Yellow stomach' smacks more of a tropical disease than a local colloquialism.

It would seem reasonable to place its true origin back to that point in time where it was first mentioned. And that all the other 'origins' are merely stage dressings which emphasise the fact already established. But when was the first mention? It has been suggested that it stems from medieval times when astrology played an important part in the conduct of affairs. In the Lincoln coat-of-arms the yellow (or golden) fleur-de-lis would represent the sun in the zodiacal sign Virgo . . . and Virgo ruling the belly we have, *ipso facto*, yellow belly. All very fine if it were just Lincoln involved, but it is a county matter, isn't it?

The next earliest mention was with regard to the Lincolnshire regiment which was formed circa 1685. In 1751, they changed their unique blue coats for scarlet ones with bright yellow facings. The gallant 10th Foot had for their colours the cross of St George upon a canary coloured ground, and retained them until 1881. So what more likely than the cry of, 'Here come the Lincolnshire Yellow-bellies' when they went into battle? But hold. Things are not quite so simple.

The Lincolnshire mail coach ran from about 1785 until 1871 and a gentleman by the name of Swinburne tells us his son was shown the original Lincolnshire Yellow-belly, a coach which he described as having been painted a dark blue, with the bodywork a canary yellow. Another gentleman by the name of Connell was assured that it was an appellation given by cockneys to the Lincolnshire to London stage coach drivers who habitually wore the longish yellow waistcoats which effectively distinguished them from the drivers from other parts of the country.

From here on in things begin to build up. A Doctor Felton tells us that the ague was very common in the Lincolnshire Fens about this time, and the chief symptoms were the protuberance of the abdomen and the yellow colour of the skin. The sufferers were described as being 'yeller as a guinea!' Also in the Fens we have the frog, Rana Temporaria, known as the Yellow Belly and anyone coming from the Fens was likewise dubbed. Then again the name is said to derive from the miners of the old iron stone quarry at Greetwell. When they emerged at the end of a shift they were liberally de-daubed with the iron-stone dust. And so the enigma goes on.

Roy Fisk, Lincolnshire Medley, *pp. 28-29.*

Dire warnings

The word 'Irby' means village of the Irish, and whether this be but a coincidence we cannot say for sure … but they do say that the old ash wood there … boggards … hauntings. You understand? And should you intend visiting Scremby with affairs which might possibly keep you abroad at a late hour, we do earnestly beg you to keep a watchful eye open for the headless bride who sometimes walks there at midnight. Not a pretty sight, we are told.

Neither is Byard's Leap near Cranwell, a place to linger by on certain blustery dark nights for, if you half incline your head you will hear, as if borne upon no earthly wind, the frightful whinnyings of a mare, the sound of which will freeze the very marrow in your bones, and set you wishing for a hot toddy and a warm fireside.

Furthermore, should misfortune direct your ways by Hardwick Hill, and you believe you see a shadowy figure upon horseback calling 'Stand and deliver!', for pity's sake we beg of you, stand not upon ceremony but fly for your life. This is none other than the notorious Dicky Rainforth, still plying his nefarious trade even beyond the grave.

Neither is it wise to venture down Bob Garth, by Kirton Lindsey, without immediate access to a hip flask primed with some stimulant, not, you understand, for the dripping figure of the lady from the Moat House, for she has been past all earthly help for goodness knows how many years now, but for yourself … you understand?

And should you pause at the black gate down Greyingham Lane and wonder that the grass has ceased to grow in one particular place, then cease your wondering. Some poor wretch was murdered there.

Then again, should some urgent business direct your steps down Saxilby way, do, we entreat you most earnestly, avoid as you would the plague, the dread Tom Otter's Lane upon the anniversary of the murder of his wife of one day. To me committed the dastardly deed here, and here his body swung in irons, screeching as it moved back and forth in the chill wind.

Roy Fisk, Lincolnshire Medley, *p. 102.*

Weather

The weather on New Year's Day was regarded as very important. Frost and snow was considered seasonal but a mild, wet day was deplored: 'Under water dearth, Under snow bread.'

The wind on New Year's Eve is also regarded as foretelling the coming season.

> If on New Year's Eve the wind blows south,
> It betokens warmth and growth.
> If west, much milk and fish in the sea,
> If north, much cold and storms will be,
> If east, the trees will bear much fruit,
> If north-east, flee it man and brute.

> A dry spring is generally followed by a rainy autumn.
> A wet spring is a sign of dry weather for harvest.
> A late spring never deceives.
> A wet Good Friday and Saturday
> Bring plenty of grass but little hay.

When the clouds form like a long boat across the sky it is said, 'Noah's Ark is out' and denotes rain. When sheep lie in the late morning before they commence to graze, it betokens a fine day:

> Many a cloudy morn, they say,
> Turns out a fine, sunshiny day,
> When the wind is in the east
> It is neither good for man nor beast,
> But when the wind is in the south
> It bows the bait in the fish's mouth.

> Rain from the south prevents drought,
> But rain from the west is always best.

> When the rain comes out of the east.
> 'Twill rain twice twenty-four hours at least.

> When the wind is in the north-west,
> The weather then is at its best.

John Ketteringham, A Lincolnshire Hotchpotch, (1989), pp. 13 and 30.

9 · FELONS, CROOKS AND CRIME

Brawling in Stamford

Lincolnshire's local newspapers contains fascinating pieces about the misdoings of the population. I dipped into some old copies of The Lincoln, Rutland and Stamford Mercury, *a newspaper still going strong although now only covering Stamford and the surrounding area and yet still the oldest paid-for weekly newspaper in the country.*

The further back you search, the more interesting (and often verbose) the writing becomes, and some of the pieces reveal as much about the character of the writers as they do what about they are describing. Most of the extracts I have included come from issues of The Mercury *in the 1830s and 1840s. There is no better way to begin than with a letter to the Editor.*

Sir, - As the object of your widely circulated journal appears to be directed to the independent advocacy of public good in general, and to the well-merited censure of abuses, I beg leave to call attention, through it, to a very great neglect of duty (as it seems to me) on the part of the police of Stamford. When the public contribute to the maintenance of a number of persons to be the guardians of the peace and order of the community, and when, not withstanding, the most shameful scenes of riot and tumult nightly disgrace our streets, it appears justifiable to question their efficiency. Probably in no town in England does the nuisance of midnight brawling prevail to a greater degree than this. In vain do the peaceful and industrious, in some parts of it, seek for repose after the toil of the day: the quiet, which ought to accompany the dark hour that nature seems to have allotted for universal repose, is broken by the harsh accents of blasphemy and obscenity; and the degrading scenes of drunkenness which are enacting under cover of darkness, send forth the sounds of those low revellings which speak loudly of a demoralising system, tolerated by those whose duty it is to see order observed, and to protect public decency. I cannot but think that the Chief Magistracy of this town was allowed to fall rather injudiciously on the very worthy and respectable person who at present holds that high and responsible office; because I think one engaged in the business which our worthy Mayor follows, is not the person most likely to be referred to for the suppression of the nuisance of an ill-conditioned public-house. It is well known that one of a most notorious character is a very profitable source of his wealth. I have addressed you, Mr. Editor, with the sole view of effecting a good, which I am sure is much desired: I am also sure that the publication of this letter will be gratefully acknowledged by very many respectable and orderly inhabitants.

Your's,

A LOVER OF GOOD ORDER

St Peter's Street, Aug 7, 1839

Berating the Clergy

The following shows the anonymous writer, perhaps the editor, using the death of a regular criminal to rant at what he perceives as the failings of the clergy.

Mr Coroner Hitchins held on Saturday last an inquest on the body of Thomas Smith, a felon, who died in the city prison on Friday. Verdict, *natural death...* Deceased had been a dissolute character, and premature death was owing to his depraved habits. Last February,

whilst enduring imprisonment for theft, he attempted to destroy himself: his term of imprisonment shortly afterwards expired; but on the 6th of March he was again convicted of felony and sentenced to three months' imprisonment. He was taken ill during this term, and on the 10th of June, the day after the expiration of the sentence, was removed to the County Hospital. In October he was again convicted of felony, and sentenced to seven years' transportation. Declining health, induced by his excesses, preventing his removal to the hulks, he remained in the city gaol. It is currently reported that the Chaplain of this prison had not for several weeks visited the deceased; and a letter to the Magistrates had been forwarded by a relative of the dead convict, praying them to enquire why a minister of the gospel, who takes a salary for doing duty at the prison, neglected to administer spiritual consolation to the man. The Rev. Gent takes 100*l.* as head-master of the Grammar-school, in return for which he teaches *one* boy, and 51*l.* a year as prison-chaplain, for which he seems disposed to make his duty equally burdensome with his school occupation; and yet he can sleep soundly on his bed: conscience sits so lightly that he has swollen to skin-bursting obesity, - or, as he said of himself when he fell over his horse when attempting to mount, "a fine large nut for the devil to crack!" – Here is a sample of the hard-working divines, who, when we friendlily admonish them to a course of duty which alone can save from the effects of the "reformation" their laziness is bringing about, taunt us with enmity to religion! And talk about the "arduous duties" of the clergy, and their "zeal for education!" Heaven gift with a glimmering of common sense the man who, when he attempts to defend his friends, pours forth upon them a flood of the bitterest irony. The literary Leviathan, Professor Wilson, has devoted a few pages of the *British Magazine* to counteract our attempts to make the clergy honest to themselves and mankind, and denounced us with all the sincerity of "good pay!" The ravings of a Scotch parasite will never slacken our zeal for religion and the real interests of the clergy: the fawning sycophant is a greater enemy than the open rebuker – and *that* the clergy will learn from the contempt they are evoking; for the time is fast coming when no spiritual magnate will lift up his voice and exclaim with Dr Etchard, "Thank God, there is ignorance enough still amongst the laity to support the authority of the clergy!"
January 10th, 1840.

Beware

The Mercury was not averse to warning its readers of the perils of lending money to foreigners, or of those who failed to pay their bills.

Hint to tradesmen. – A tall, morose-looking man, about 60 years of age, and his wife, far advanced in pregnancy, about 38 years of age, very bold, red looking, rather handsome, and pleasing in conversation, have resided in Newark and the neighbourhood for some time, and have made a move towards Gainsboro' or Hull without paying their tradesmen's bills. They have with them two children, a boy and a girl.
January 26th, 1821

Caution. – The tradespeople of Stamford have been much incensed this week by the sudden absence of a Frenchman, (a pseudo (Chevalier') who has been here for a few months as a teacher of languages. He had by plausible manners, contrived to borrow money of some, and got otherwise into debt of money.
May 8th, 1818

Vagrancy

Lincoln at this juncture is overrun with vagrants: the various parish officers, notwithstanding several thousand mendacity-tickets have been issued by the Union, refuse to send applicants for relief to the house, lest the person sent should become ill or die, in which event the expense would be chargeable to the particular parish from which he was sent: the guardians refuse to confederate the various parishes to bear the expense jointly. Yesterday it was complained, at the Magistrates' meeting, that several distressed persons had been permitted to remain in the streets by the parish-officers, rather than risk sending them to the Union. The Magistrates directed the police-inspector to accompany any vagrant to the parish-officer who had first refused him relief, and if the officer still persisted in not granting it, to lay as information against him. – Thursday next was fixed conditionally, if the prison-Chaplain should return home in the interval, for an inquiry into his conduct.
January 10th, 1840.

Drunken Frolics

Last market-day, two persons who were riding up the High-street, intoxicated, galloped so furiously as to endanger the lives of several persons who were crossing the street. Near St Botolph's Green they came in collision with the ass and cart of a poor cripple who obtains a livelihood by coal-leading: the concussion killed the poor fellow's ass upon the spot. Cannot the Magistracy punish for such drunken freaks, and compel the offenders to make reparation for their aggression? Or has the poor man no other remedy than an appeal by action?

January 10th, 1840.

The Thimble-rig Gentry

Half a dozen of the thimble-rig gentry honoured Lincoln with their presence last market-day: two of the fraternity, who were found sitting on Crosscliff-hill with legs akimbo, inviting comers to the market to hazard their cash, were taken under the protection of the police force, and by the magistrates were sent to Lob's pound, to experience a month's hospitality at the expense of the city.

January 10th, 1840.

Playing Chuck

Sunday was originally a day of rest and anyone who disturbed the peace was punished. This usually meant a few hours in the stocks and was given mainly for 'breaking the Sabbath' by drinking or gambling. 'Chuck' was probably a game of tag. My oldest dictionary, of 1899, gives chuck as a verb meaning to strike gently, or as a noun meaning a slight blow. In effect, Daniels and Smith were messing around.

On Monday John Daniels and William Smith, peddlers, were exposed in the stocks for three hours for playing at chuck within the liberties of this [Stamford] borough on Sunday the 12th ult.

May 8th, 1818.

Robbery

GAINSBORO'. – One of the most impudent robberies committed in this town for many years took place on Thursday night, the 21st ult. On the premises of Mr Herriatt, at the Black Bull in Lord-street. The thieves had to scale three or four very high walls before they could arrive at the house: this was accomplished by placing a ladder, and then pulling it up after them, and so on to the next wall. Having come at length to the back door, an entrance was made by taking out a square of glass and unfastening the kitchen window. Afterwards the back door was thrown open, and a quart measure full of ale was placed against it to keep it open: the thieves barricaded the lodging-room where the landlord was asleep, by placing a quantity of chairs and other furniture against the door, and then commenced ransacking almost every cupboard and drawer in the house, and stealing all that was valuable and easily to be removed. The robbery was obviously the work of one well acquainted with the premises, as not a door was disturbed which led to any apartment not likely to have that description of property. The following silver articles have been missed, viz., a snuff box, cream jug with the freemason's coat of arms engraved on it, pair of spectacles, five table-spoons, eight tea-spoons, pair of sugar bows, and a caddie spoon. The drawers and cupboards were forced open with a chisel belonging to Mr Herriatt, and which must have been procured prior to the thieves' obtaining entrance into the house, as the store-room where it was always kept was discovered to be locked after the robbery.
March 1st, 1839.

Mischief

For some time past a horde of wantonly mischievous boys have nightly annoyed the residents in Guildhall-street, by ringing the door bells and thundering at the knockers. A surgeon, on whom the trick had been frequently practised, hit upon a capital expedient for detecting the runaway plagues: getting his electrical apparatus into order, he charged the leyden jar rather powerfully, and communicated it with the bell-wire. Scarcely had he done so, when the bell rang, and

on opening the door a juvenile delinquent was found prostrated all his length by the shock, and calling out lustily. The young scamp was nearly frightened out of his senses; and after a sound lecturing, he was permitted to depart without further punishment.
September 27th, 1839.

The Genteel Begging Nuisance

The practice of *ladies* begging money from door to door has become an intolerable nuisance in Boston. A correspondent writes thus – "Last week furnished a fair specimen of this bore. On Monday *two* pale-faced *ladies* tapped at my door, who wished "Missus" to sign a very impudently severe reprimand to our illustrious Queen for allowing that naughty man, Robert Owen, to appear in court! It happened that "Missus" was born on Mr. Owen's estate in New Lanark, and therefore not only knew that Mr. Owen was the esteemed friend of the late Duke of Kent, our sovereign's illustrious parent, but was cognisant of Mr. Owen's charities to the tune of 15,000*l.* annually. Application of course refused.

Tap second: *two ladies* again, who wish for a subscription to the Primitive Methodist New Chapel. Gave five shillings. Tap third: *Two ladies* (for these fair solicitors always hunt in couples) solicit a subscription to the Zion Sunday school. Gave sixpence. Tap fourth: *Two ladies* again, who wish for a subscription to the Wesleyan cause. Here is a pretty modest request; the husbands of these identical ladies having, with other Wesleyan Methodists, expelled correspondent from a society of which he was a consistent member and a zealous supporter, on the ground that he was an infidel with whom they could hold no intercourse!"
September 27th, 1839.

The Lincolnshire Poacher

Crime is often depicted in song and one of the most famous traditional English folk songs comes from Lincolnshire. Poaching in the nineteenth century was a serious crime and punishable by death. This is, I think, the best known version of the song.

When I was bound apprentice in famous Lincolnshire
  Full well I served my master, for more than seven year,
Till I took up to poaching as you shall quickly hear,
  Oh, 'tis my delight on a shiny night
 In the season of the year.

As me and my companions were setting of a snare,
  'Twas then we spied the gamekeeper, for him we did not care,
For we can wrestle and fight, my boys, and jump o'er anywhere.
  Oh, 'tis my delight on a shiny night
  In the season of the year.

As me and my companions were setting four or five,
  And taking on 'em up again, we caught a hare alive,
We took the hare alive, my boys, although the wood did steer.
  Oh, 'tis my delight on a shiny night
  In the season of the year.

I threw him on my shoulder and then we all trudged home,
  We took him to a neighbour's house and sold him for a crown,
We sold him for a crown, my boys, but I need not tell you where!
  Oh, 'tis my delight on a shiny night
  In the season of the year.

Success to every gentleman that lives in Lincolnshire,
  Success to every poacher that wants to sell a hare.
Bad luck to every gamekeeper that will not sell his deer.
  Oh, 'tis my delight on a shiny night
  In the season of the year.

Roy Fisk makes the following comments.

The song itself has been traced back to 1776 but might belong to an even earlier date. It is the most famous of all the county songs and not only is it the signature tune for Radio Lincolnshire, its rousing chorus has been sung wherever Yellow Bellies have travelled in the world. It was also, we are told, a great favourite with George IV and he used to have it sung for his own amusement. He also commanded to have it sung at his harvest homes.

But poaching was not really the romantic business it was made out to be; it was fraught with danger and discomfort and the penalties for those caught were harsh. When one considers that a labourer's wages at this point in time was only 8d a day, it is not very surprising that he had to resort to poaching to eke out his meagre meat ration and pittance of a wage.

Whilst there appears to be no story attached to the song, it can be no exaggeration there must be thousands of stories worth relating about the Lincolnshire Poacher as such, and his nocturnal escapades in search of game. One such story was told to us personally by Gaffer, a character not unknown to the local bobby as a poacher. He was pushing his ancient bike up Burton Hill one evening with his poacher's pocket bulging in a most satisfying fashion, and had reached the summit when he spotted the Law ... a dark silhouette in the moonlight. Gaffer promptly turned up the wick of his oil lamp until the top of it glowed a cherry red, then he blew it out as he turned the corner.

" 'ello, 'ello, 'ello!" said the Law. "Wot's this then, Gaffer? No lights, hey?"

"Well it was lit a moment ago officer," replied Gaffer, innocently. Whereupon the Law clapped an exploratory hand upon the top of the lamp to see whether it was still warm. It was. Very! There was a sudden scream and this particular arm of the law began thrashing its own particular arm about in the most unlawful-like manner. Gaffer, with a smile of quiet satisfaction, remounted his bike and pedalled off with a polite "G'nite, officer."

Roy Fisk, Lincolnshire Medley, pp. 100-101.

The Court of Quarter Sessions

Four times each year, at Epiphany (January), Easter (April), Midsummer (July) and Michaelmas (October), the active magistrates met in quarter sessions. In Lindsey it needs only a little imagination to see these eighteenth-century courts. The old buildings still stand in Spital in the Street, the courthouse bearing an inscription which has been translated as:

This court does right,

Loves Peace,

Preserves the Laws,

Rewards the righteous cause.

In several of the sessions towns the market squares retain the pattern of two centuries ago. Spilsby is a good example. The plain eighteenth-century town hall where sessions were held still stands in the middle of the rectangular market place. Just across the square from it is the imposing White Hart inn to which the magistrates adjourned in the afternoon to deal with administrative business. Between the two was a convenient space where some of the floggings took place at the rising of the court.

The importance and success of the sessions were reflected by the enormous numbers of people who attended. Even in this thinly populated area where each sessions might be adjourned to as many as six little towns each meeting required a huge, bustling concourse of people. They crowded the inns and packed the market squares, urgent for the ten o'clock start. There were magistrates and their clerks arriving in coaches, perhaps with some servants; also in a coach was the clerk of the peace with his deputies, books and papers; there were attorneys and their assistants; high constables (usually two from each wapentake); petty constables (one from each parish); local officials like treasurers and surveyors of the highways; sheriff's bailiffs, anxiously checking to see if all the jurors they had summoned had turned up; and the jurors themselves, at least sixteen for the grand jury, and a dozen or so for a petty jury.

Then there were the prosecutors, determined to solve the often long-running feuds which had eventually driven them to law, marshalling their witnesses; and finally there were the accused, the lucky ones travelling from their homes to answer to their bonds. The less fortunate were brought from the house of correction by cart or on foot, but often in chains, led by the keeper of the house. In his cart he also carried some of the weightier legal tomes needed at sessions and a selection of his cats o' nine tails, for it was one of his duties to flog offenders at the end of the proceedings. In all, anything over one hundred people must have attended. Sessions day was a grand and turbulent occasion in the lives of these towns and their surrounding districts.

All this hustle and bustle, the spontaneity and colour of early morning on sessions day in Spilsby, tended to confirm some magistrates' views of the chaotic state of the lower orders. It was not a reasonable system of government in the modern sense. Modern systems expect major and unceasing changes to be the order of things; the emphasis is on individual rights, especially people's right to 'get on with their own lives'; government is active at many levels and is supported by a vast professional bureaucracy. If a problem occurs it is expected that the professional politicians and their officials will develop a new policy to deal with it.

The eighteenth-century system was very different but it was coherent and effective. The central idea which held the whole system together was the notion of the king's peace, a constant, unchanging and perfect order, which was the duty of every citizen to uphold. If an assault took place, the king's peace had been broken and it was the duty of the victim to bring proceedings; if a road was out of repair it was the duty of the parish to restore the king's highway to the standard required by His Majesty. Without a busy bureaucracy offenders were not vigorously pursued, but once a breach of the king's peace had been recorded, the system was relentless and implacable in keeping the culprit bound to appear before the king's justices and make restitution.

B.J. Davey, Rural Crime in the Eighteenth Century: North Lincolnshire 1740-80, (1994), pp. 80-82.

Breaking the Sabbath

Letter to Mr Thos Boar of Crowland
Dr. Sir,
If you have the Act of Parliament against Sabbath Breaking, [I] shall take it a kind favour for the use of it [for] a few minutes. I am very lame or would have come but hope I shall be able to attend the Vestry to give my feeble voice against one of the greatest of Sins.
Your abt. sert.
Wm M Marker
Quarter Sessions Records, Crowland Par 12/6, letter.

Wife-Selling

When Thomas Hardy wrote The Mayor of Casterbridge *he began with a scene of a man selling his wife. Notebooks of Hardy's recently discovered show that, like many novelists today, he took some of his ideas from newspapers. Between 1668 and 1857 divorce was only possible by bringing a Private Member's Bill to the House of Lords so the practice of selling a wife was virtually the only way the poor could obtain a separation. Hardy's information came initially from the* Rutland, Lincoln and Stamford Mercury *and was reported again in the* Dorset County Chronicle *a week later.*

The disgraceful scene of a fellow's selling and delivering his wife was exhibited at Stamford market on Friday last [18th September 1829]. The price obtained was four shillings! Robert Phillips, under-ostler at the George inn, was the seller, and a man named Wm. Brown, a labourer of Oakham was the purchaser. They were permitted to retire from the market-hill without molestation.
Stamford Mercury, 25th *September 1829*

Reward for Capture

Stamford Sunday, Jan 31 1813

Whereas John Palmer, Carrier, was attacked by Three Footpads about 5 o'clock this Morning, on the Highway, near Thorpe's Mill, at Market Deeping, one of whom fired a Pistol Ball through the Flashy Part of Palmer's left Arm; he notwithstanding defended himself against the Three Villains, who tried, without Effect, to pull him out of his cart, but he resolutely fought them with a pistol (which would not go off) and threatened to shoot them on which they ran away.

A Woman Passenger, (Mrs Parr, of Deeping, and her Infant) who was sitting by the Side of Palmer, had her eye-brows singed by the Priming of the Villain's Pistol. Between the hours of 8 and 10 o'clock, Three Men came to The New Inn at Market Deeping, on foot; one was a tall, thin Man, with large Whiskers, a dark Great Coat, and Boots; one a low, stout Man, with a light Pair of Small-clothes, Boots, and a dark Great Coat: these Two were an Hour and a Half before the other Man came: the last Man (who never sat down) was of a middling Size, and had a dark Great Coat and Gaiters. They left the House about 10 o'clock on Saturday Night.

These Three Men are suspected to be the same Persons who stopped Palmer.

Whoever will discover the Offender or Offenders, so they may be prosecuted to Conviction, shall receive a Reward of TEN GUINEAS from the said John Palmer, at The Royal Oak, Stamford, over and above the Reward of FORTY POUNDS allowable by Act of Parliament.

If any one of them will impeach his accomplices, he shall be intitled the above Reward, and every endeavour used to obtain his Pardon.

Newcomb & Sons, Printers, Stamford

Quarter Sessions Records, Crowland Par 12/5, Public Notice.

10 · SMUGGLING AND PIRATES

The Heyday of Smuggling

The secluded creeks of the Lincolnshire coast were ideal for those wanting to deal in contraband goods. Sneaking out on a moonless night with bales of the county's fine wool, horses' hooves and cart wheels muffled with sacking and straw, the smugglers edged along the coast, mindful of the revenue officers patrolling the shore-line. The boats were signalled, the booty transferred. In return for prized Lincolnshire wool, smugglers brought back tobacco, Dutch gin and brandy, fine silks and tea – at one time all highly taxed in England.

Smuggling of some kind has always taken place somewhere along the ragged coast of Lincolnshire but it was especially common in the seventeenth and eighteenth centuries.

The night was dark but not stormy. Jack Anderson, the new farm labourer, hired by Ben Oliver at Louth Stattus fair, and Ned, who knew what it was all about, were ordered to get the horses and carts ready. It was a short distance from the farm to Oliver's Gap north of

Mablethorpe, the soft sand deadening the sound of wheels, and then across the wide beach towards the sea. When the gently lapping water was up to the bellies of the horses and the body of the cart they turned the carts round with the horses' heads towards land, and waited. Presently, a small Dutch galliot sailed quietly alongside. Kegs and bales were transferred. Until the cart was full, and the vessel slid away to the next cart. As the carts lumbered slowly but silently over a gap in the sandhills, the carts of other neighbours passed by almost unseen in the moonless night. The organisation had been good and there was no Riding Officer of the Preventative Service about. It was a successful night for smugglers.

A few nights later the horses were again harnessed, the white face of one covered with sacking, and the cart wheels wrapped in straw, and some old sacks containing sea sand were put in the cart just in case the straw wore off the wheels. They had to traverse some rough chalk and gravel roads across the Marsh and the noise of iron-shod wheels could carry some distance and arouse suspicions. Before morning the gin and tobacco would be safely stowed away in cottage chimneys, barns and even rectory cellars.

The hey-day of smuggling, or contraband trading, was in the eighteenth and first half of the nineteenth centuries. The vast increase in customs duty on tea, spirits, tobacco and silk made it profitable to 'import' them without paying duty. A tax could also be levied on exports, or penalties imposed for illegal export. When there was an embargo on the export of wool in 1274-75, William de Len and certain other Louth men sold 200 sacks of wool to Flemish merchants, and got them away by ship from Saltfleet and Suine with the aid of bribes, including a cask of wine for Alan of Conisholme. Later, under an act of 1672, the export of wool was prohibited; increasing amounts of wool unsold in the county and the demand from the Continent led to smuggling; the Lincolnshire coast, with its gently shelving sands and secluded creeks, was well suited for the purpose. The wool smugglers, who only worked at night and were known as 'owlers', operated from marshland villages near the coast like Irby in the Marsh near Wainfleet, and small boats put out from Grainthorpe and Saltfleet to meet ships out at sea. It was said that few ships left a Lincolnshire port without one or two sacks of wool, perhaps labelled 'hops', surreptitiously stowed in the hold.

In 1785 no less than 90 tons of wool were put aboard a vessel at Goxhill Haven in the Humber estuary, for export to Dunkirk. That same year the first Stuff Ball was held, at Alford, as an attempt to stimulate interest in the manufacturing of wool in the county, and two years earlier the philanthropic rector of Theddlethorpe and Willoughby, Rev. Reynold Gideon Bouyer, started local spinning schools. But these and other measures did little to check the smugglers. And what was more natural than to organise a return cargo? The smuggling out of wool suffered a decline when the already harsh penalties for illegal export, including flogging, transportation and hanging, were increased in the late 1780s, and the efficiency of the preventative services improved. But the smuggling of imports was already well established, and continued after prohibition of wool export was removed in 1825. In fact, so much Dutch gin or hollands was smuggled into Dent's Creek on the Humber, in kegs and bladders sometimes weighted and hidden in the creek itself, that it became known as New Holland.

David N. Robinson, The Book of the Seaside, (1981), pp. 45-46.

Pirates in the Humber

You can sense Edward Peacock's disapproval and outrage in this account of how people he considered highly respectable became involved with such low life. As his diatribe continues, he appears to become obsessed with the correct meaning of the word 'osmonds'.

It is a long time since our shores have been infested by pirates, though not quite so great a distance of time as some people have come to imagine. In the reign of Charles the First, pirate vessels from Algiers, Salee, and other Moslem ports of the Mediterranean, swept the British Channel, and carried off men and women into captivity. In 1637 a pamphlet was published, which has now become extremely rare, entitled, A True Journal of Sally Fleet, with the proceedings of the voyage, whereunto is annexed a list of the Sally Captives' names, and the places where they dwell.'

Long after the Salee pirates had ceased to be a serious danger, the coasts of England were troubled by vessels from Dunkirk, which not only preyed on our commerce, but occasionally committed atrocities on land. Wandering beggars were frequent in those days, who appealed to the sympathy of their fellow countrymen on the grounds that they had been pillaged by 'Dunkirkes,' the name by which these pirate vessels were known. Entries of small sums given to these sufferers are common in old churchwardens' accounts.

The most recent piratical attack from which inhabitants of these islands have suffered was during our unhappy strife with America, when Paul Jones landed in Scotland and threatened the Yorkshire coast. It may, however, be maintained that Jones was not a pirate, but a regular belligerent according to the laws of war as then interpreted.

During the latter middle ages, and far down into Tudor time, the Humber was a place subject to piratical inroads. Much curious information concerning the doings of these sea-thieves is in existence, but as yet the whole of it is locked in manuscript. We propose to draw attention to a piratical adventure in the reign of Henry VIII, which may not be without interest to both Yorkshire and Lincolnshire readers. The records of the old court of Star Chamber, as far as they are known to exist, are preserved in the National Record Office. It is from them that we have gleaned the following particulars. The evil deeds of the Humber pirates have long been known, their memory as yet exists as a vague tradition, but it is with a feeling of surprise that we find a great northern ecclesiastic – the Abbot of Whitby – engaged in questionable transactions with disreputable persons of this class. The other accomplices in these evil transactions – Ganth, Lappage, Parys and Litilprowe – we can obtain no information of. The Abbot of Whitby who, according to allegation made in the Star Chamber bill, was a part purchaser of the ship, merchandise and stores, was John Hexham, or as he was otherwise named Topcliffe. The latter name he acquired from the place of his birth, Topcliffe, near Thirsk … John and Gregory Conyers were, there can be no doubt, gentlemen of illustrious lineage, cadets of that noble tree whose branches once spread so widely over the north country. Their precise place of pedigree has not, as yet, been made out. Bosshell, Ledham and Pekok were probably Whitby townsmen who had no scruples of conscience as to doing business with pirates when the trade could be carried on safely under the shelter of the name of their abbot and of members of the great house of Conyers. We must remember, however, that the statements of the complainants is alone before us; what the reply may have been we do not know. It is lost or at least at present it is not forthcoming. Could we hear both sides, the affair might bear a widely different complexion. The inventory attached is by far the most interesting part of these old documents, as it gives us a list of the cargo and stores of the vessel. Many persons think our forefathers of three centuries ago were barbarous in almost everything that is related to the sea. They may perhaps be surprised to find that the *Jhesus* of Dantzic had on board both a pump and a compass.

We do not think it necessary to print the bill in its original language and spelling, as we edited it in that form some years ago for the *Yorkshire Archaeological and Topographical Journal*. The bill sets forth, with the usual cumberous law forms, that Henry Ganth, of 'the cite of Dansik in Aslmayn', had contracted with certain persons to carry in his ship, the *Jhesus*, twenty lasts* of rye, thirty lasts and nine barrels of meal, and three half packs* of flax, six hundred vores (oars) and six lasts of pitch as well as certain other matters, among which we find a last of osmonds.

This word is rare and has now become obsolete. Its precise meaning was long unknown. Those dictionaries in which it occurs commonly give a vague or incorrect interpretation. In Blount's Law Dictionary we are told it is 'a kind of ore or iron-stone assuming the nature of iron,' and Cowell and Jacobs say much the same. Whishaw's New Law Dictionary, published in 1829, carries on the erroneous tradition. Halliwell calls it a kind of iron, and Admiral Smyth defines it as pig-iron. It is useless to repeat the guesses, all more or less erroneous, that have been made by other dictionary-makers and annotators.

It has now been demonstrated that osmonds were not iron-ore or pig-iron, but 'the very best iron used, and probably used only for the finest purposes, such as arrow-heads, fish-hooks, the repairs of bell-gear, and the works of clocks'. It seems to have been imported into this country in small bars packed in barrels. The origin of the name has not been discovered. The late Mr. T. Hudson Turner suggested that it took its designation from the place of its manufacture, but this is almost certainly a mistake. It furnishes one more example of the folly of mere speculation in matters of philology. The term seems to have come into use in this country in the fourteenth century, and to have been well understood until the seventeenth. In the Louth churchwardens' account for 1510-1511, we read of 'osmondes to bell yokes', and in 1530 a small sum was paid to 'the clockmender for osmondes.' In the inventory of John Nevill of Faldingworth, a roll in our own possession, dated the seventh year of Edward VI, we find that he possessed 'a barrel of osmonds' which was valued at fourteen shillings.

For the carriage of these goods Ganth was to have received fifty-eight pounds of English money. Besides the ordinary cargo, Ganth had some property of his own on board. The *Jhesus* arrived safely in the Humber, where she cast anchor. There she was boarded by a French vessel, 'a shippe of Bolayn' as she is here called, and was forthwith carried to the port of Whitby, and her cargo sold by the sea-thieves to the abbot, the two Conyers, Pekok, and others, who, it is alleged, were well aware that the property was stolen. A curious inventory of the goods on board the ship – too long to reprint here – follows the petition, and then darkness settles down on this singular transaction.

We have been unable to discover the reply which must have been made by the abbot and others. It is much to be desired that further light should be thrown on the subject.

* a last of corn or rape seed is ten quarters; of pitch, tar or ashes, fourteen barrels. A pack of wool is a horse load, i.e. seventeen stone and two pounds.
William Andrews, (ed), Bygone Lincolnshire (1891) pp. 124 – 131.

Thwarting the Law

A common ruse to decoy the coastguard away from the actual landing, which worked more often than not, was to draw his attention to a mysterious boat showing a light and sailing coast-wise in the opposite direction. Or a lantern would be strapped to a horse's leg 'so that coastguards might mistake the animal for a ship riding at anchor'. On one occasion smuggler Tommy feigned to be in his cups in a pub in North Somercotes, and rambled on to the effect that if only they knew it, the coastguard of the district could capture a prize contraband the evening of that very day. It worked. The word was passed on and preventative officers from the next station of East Theddlethorpe came to reinforce the vigil. That night Tommy supervised a successful run on the unguarded coast. A rather neat trick was when a coastguard officer was 'treated' by known smugglers at a wayside Tom and Jerry (inn) and he began to boast that he could run down anyone even if it meant jumping over the gout (drain by the sluice). On being challenged to demonstrate his prowess, inevitably he failed. While he went home to change into dry clothes, another successful run was made. And of course there were some preventative officers not above taking a bribe of smuggled spirits as the price of turning a blind eye; in fact the old saying is still quoted – 'Put a guinea in each of my eyes, and I shall see nothing'. Still, could it be that the skeleton with the royal insignia brass buttons, found in 1902 in the brickwork of the Vine at Skegness, was that of a 'preventative officer' who refused such bribery?

David N. Robinson, *The Book of the Seaside*, (1981) pp. 45-46.

George Brant goes Smuggling

Not only were the creeks and marshes of the Humber and the Wash hotbeds of smuggling, further down the coast the sandy beaches and high dunes between Saltfleet and Skegness also provided ideal conditions for running a ship ashore.

In the nineteenth century there were many who either actively encouraged or turned a blind eye to attempts to avoid import duty. Amongst them, were the Marshmen, who were advocates of 'free trade'.

George Brant was born in Tetford in 1832, the son of poor Methodist parents. When he was seven he started work in a brickyard with his father and ran away to sea when he was thirteen. He seemed to be a boy who lived on his wits and he wrote of his adventures in a little black notebook in a particularly matter-of-fact way.

I was now very fond of drink. My funds were low and I did not like work. I was invited by a party of smugglers to go across to Holland to fetch a cargo of tobacco, part of it unmanufactured at sixpence per pound and the shag sevenpence per pound. We got some to our own coast and then through bad management the cargo was thrown away when there was no danger. The next time we went we had fine weather and landed safe at Malthorpe after much difficulty occasioned by the coastguards. We lost the boat a few days after. It went to pieces on the shore and another young man and I had a narrow escape for our lives. We soon went again in a better boat and landed safely at Huttoft with very little trouble. I had now plenty of money to spend and was often drinking for days together. The next time we went we had to run into Boston Deeps as we could not land on the coast. I went on shore at Frisney to arrange things, as I was acquainted with the shore. I got things all ready and showed a light, but they got the boat on shore on a sand and we could not get to them. The next night they got the boat on the same sand and were very near being drowned. They had to throw the cargo out to save their lives, but we soon went again and landed at Mumby Chapel.

The nights were getting very short so we went no more for some months. I had a nice little coal coble then and went fishing and pleasuring at Malthorpe then, and spent my money as fast as I could get it. I slept out of doors and Sundays were spent the same as other days, for I had no clothes to put on to appear decent. At the age of eighteen I associated chiefly among drunkards. I went to Holland again in August, and we had a fine passage there and part of the way back, when we were caught in a gale of wind WSW: about eleven o'clock at night. A heavy sea struck the boat and pitched her on her beam end, and half filled her with water and shifted the ballast. We thought it was all over with us. I shall never forget that awful moment when the sea struck the boat. I was asleep on some straw in the hold, and my mates were in the cuddy. I was suddenly awoke from my sleep with the stroke of the sea. We had some loose stones in the boat for ballast and the stones and myself were shifted from side to side together amongst the water. I thought, 'Another sea and the boat will go over all together and we shall be in eternity.' For a few moments I tried to pray but the heavens were like brass to my prayers. I tried to find my way out of that place but could not. One of my comrades called out to me and I answered. As soon as we found out how we were fixed we started clearing the boat of the water and packing the ballast up to the windward, and lowered the mast and so got the boat right again. We then let her go to the mercy of the waves for two days. The third night the wind changed to SE and we reached the land safely at Skegness. We put a man ashore to make all ready for landing our cargo. It came on misty so we could not see the signal. So we had to run from the land and we ran very near a revenue cutter before we saw it. The mist was so thick they did not suspect us. We had to run up Boston Deeps for fear of suspicion. The Wainfleet coastguard men saw us and got their boat back of the sands and were nearly to us before we saw them. They fired a gun for us to lay to. We had a deal of work to do in a little time. We turned our boat with her broadside towards them and put the cargo out on the opposite side. When their boat came along side of us we smelt very strongly of tobacco, but that was all, for it had gone to the deeps. My companion and myself both looked very rough. We each of us had a stocking on our heads for we had lost our sou-wester hats in the gale, and had not had a fire since the squall came on, for we had all our matches spoilt and our fire put out, and we were nearly lost with dirt.

The coastguard men went back, and had scarcely got away when the revenue cutter came and took our boat from us for not having a licence. They talked to taking us to Grimsby, but after putting us about a good deal they let us go. I now thought I would not go across to Holland any more. I left my master W Dales. We went twice more, got one cargo safe and lost the other. He then went again and too three men more with him. They were all married and had families. One of them marries Dales's daughter. They have not been seen or heard of since. It is of the general opinion that they were lost on the Dutch coast in a gale of wind from the NW.

J E Swaby, The Marshmen, (1962) p. 76-78.

A Boston Smuggler of the 1920s

In the cosy bar of the 'Loggerheads' down by Constitution Wharf, I found to my surprise a goodly company of the fraternity gathered about a picturesque figure, with ear-rings and flowing locks and a great sea-cape thrown loosely over his broad shoulders. His face was tanned a deep mahogany from exposure to the sun and wind in the tropics, and I concluded, from some long voyage.

So he had, but a voyage of such amazing character – such a noteworthy adventure – that I make no apology for giving a somewhat lengthy description thereof. Here before me stood Sir Francis Drake's successor – a boon companion of those who sailed with Captain Flint and Long John Silver – a modern twentieth-century pirate.

'Yaas,' he was saying, as I entered unobtrusively and took my seat at a beer-stained table near the group, taking care, however, to mix with two or three others, also obviously interested in the coming yarn. 'I went all right. At first I didn't 'alf like the job, seein' as ow we stood as good a chance of bein' copped by them fast police boats as ever I know. 'Owever, the money was worth it. When we got to the coast – or rather to Rum Row – I was put, with two others, on a motor-boat – the *Helena* she were – an' the job was to run a cargo ashore by Salvation Point. Me an' Bob 'Arris an' Sam Tallweather were all together; it warn't the fust time we'd done a job neither. My! But it took a nerve! Black as a winter midnight in the Arctic it were when we shoved off from the *Astor* wi' our cargo o' rum and ran straight as a die for the Point. That name *Astor* was a bit of a joke like. Cap'n told me the ship were named arter Lasy Astor by a Scotch merchant wot ' ad bought 'er – 'e 'ad some humour, eh? – an' t'were silent as a grave when we ran the *Helena* high an' dry on the beach.

'While the lorry crew set to work unloadin' the barrels Bob an' me an' Saaam were told off, wi' revolvers, to guard agin surprise. As a sea-farin' man, I reckon I can use a six-shooter as quick as most. Anyway, there we were, an' the Customs men might come on us at any moment. The loadin' was quick and quiet enough, an' a big fellow supervised. I didn't like the looks of 'im , I can tell yer. Narrow, Squintin' eyes, 'e 'ad. an' a low forehead – leastways wot I could see of it. Howsomever, I see a light on the foreshore, sudden like, an' I say to Sam an' Bob: ' 'Ere,' I sez, 'what be that light yonder?' none o' us liked investigatin'; but that was our job; an' anyway, the others were too busy loadin' the lorry to see anythin' else.

'Well, we cut up the beach, an' I'm blowed if we didn't find ourselves in a garden; yaas, a blessed garden wi' an 'ouse an' all attached. We could 'ear music an' the sound o' dancin' through the open winders, an we ventured nearer to see wot it all were. At that moment a tall chap, wi' a black patch over his eye an' a scar on 'is face stepped out on to the lawn an' lit a cigar.

'Just then a girl joined ' im, an' I'm blessed if they two didn't start makin' love right in front of us. Yaas – under a tree by that winder – there they was a-kissin' an' a-cuddlin' all they knew 'ow. That's wot led to our trouble, 'cause the silly chump took a flask out o' his pocket an' offered the girl a drink. She didn't 'alf accept either – these Yanks know a good thing when they see it – there war'nt no lemonade in that flask believe me – an' Bob 'Arris, through leanin' forward to smell what it were, lost 'is balance an' right bang on that lawn. They started up like as they'd bin shot; but we was quicker, an' was coverin' them in a jiffy. 'Now then,' I sez, quick and businesslike, 'up wi' your 'ands, an' not a sound, or you're both dead 'uns.' They were too astonished to protest or to say anything, while Bob 'e picked 'isself up, an' looked mighty foolish. Just then a voice came out o' the 'ouse callin' everybody to supper; an' I sez agin, ' 'Ere, tell 'em as you'll be along in a few minutes; quick now, or – '. You should 'ave seen their faces. 'Owever, they 'and't got no chance; so the chap 'e calls out loud as I tells 'im. 'Now then,' 'e says quietly, 'wot's this, a hold-up?'

' 'No,' I sez, ' it ain't yet, but it mighty soon will be, if you give the game away. You're to stop 'ere, an' if you move, you're a dead 'un.' With that we tied him up an' the girl too. An' started off back to the ship. But we' and't reckoned on a Yank knowin' conjurin' tricks wi' knots; an' before you could say Jack Robinson 'e was arter us. Not that we heard 'im coming – 'e was too artful for that; but just as we got to the beach we turned an' saw 'im standin' by the garden wall, an' o' course 'e could see the lorry an' the boat an' all.

'Quick as thought we fired; but 'e dodged, an' we 'eard voices callin' an' the rattle of arms as men pored out o' the ' ouse. Shouts of 'freebooters,' 'pirates,' came to us as we rushed down the shingle to where the last cases were bein' loaded up. Well, the long an' short of it was, we pushed off there an' then wi' the last three cases still in the boat. The lorry started off at full speed past the ' ouse, were we 'eard some shots fired, an' we saw the bootlegging Johnny and his pals advance towards the garden, shooting as they went. Our job was to get the remainder of the rum back to the *Astor* 'fore the police boats copped us; an' it wor a race I tell yer. Two on 'em suddenly rounded a peninsula an' chased us at full speed. 'Owever, the Helena were a good boat, an' we just got outside the limit as the foremost police launch came into range. Even then some bullets whistled over us; but we were darned glad to be able to shake our fists an' get back to the *Astor* wot was waiting, anxious enough like through hearin' the firin' an' all. We 'eard arterwards as 'ow the bootlegger an' his pals 'ad driven all the party into the 'ouse an' locked them up. Then they'd made merry wi' the victuals, an' got away at dawn, wi'out a trace. Ah! Lads; it's a great game this rum-running; but a thirsty one, you bet. Thanks; I'll ha' a quart, arter that.'

With which, he beamed around on the awe-stricken faces of the company, solemnly drained his two pint tankards at a gulp each, filled a short clay pipe, and settled himself comfortably, as a man who has earned his repose after a day of labour.

Christopher Marlowe, The Fen Country, *(1925), pp. 142-256.*

11 · MEDICAL MATTERS

The Black Death in Lincolnshire

The Black Death is thought to have originated in central Asia, affecting China in the early 1330s, spreading through the Crimea and into the Italian trading ports during the following decade, eventually arriving on the south-west coast of England by June or July 1348. It infiltrated the populations of Asia Minor, North Africa, the whole of Europe, and even Greenland, killing millions of people before it ran its course. Mediaeval writers speak of boils or buboes suddenly appearing in the groin or armpits preceding a rash of black spots on various parts of the body, symptoms which indicate infection from the bacillus Pasteurella Pestis.

We know from the evidence of the Louth Park *Chronicle* that the Black Death dealt Lincolnshire a cruel blow, significantly reducing its population:

This scourge in so many places left less than a fifth part of the population surviving . . . So great a pestilence before this time had never been seen, or heard of, or written of; for it is believed that not even so vast a multitude of people were swept away by the flood which happened in the days of Noe . . . In the year many monks of Louth Park died. Among them died Walter of Louth, Lord Abbot.

There is no way of knowing precisely how high the mortality rate was in Lincolnshire between the beginning of 1349 and 1350. The document most resembling a survey of the period is the register of John Gynewell, the bishop of Lincoln at the time. It does not record deaths in the villages (we must wait until the sixteenth century for the parish registers to preserve this information) but it does contain details of mortality among incumbents within the diocese. If a vacancy arose for a vicar, rector or chaplain in one of his parishes, the bishop had to approve whoever was presented to succeed in the office, the details – including the reason for the vacancy – being recorded in the register. There was certainly a very high number of vacancies throughout the diocese caused by the incumbent's death, and nowhere more than in Lincolnshire. During the year 25 March 1349 to 1350, 44.84% of the 533 benefices in the archdeaconry of Lincoln and 57.14% of 98 benefices in the archdeaconry of Stow fell vacant. This is clearly no accurate guide to the general mortality rate since the clergy may have been more liable to infection than other occupational groups. However, the figures are a dramatic reflection on the Black Death's widespread impact, and where the priest fell victim others in the village almost certainly did too.

Graham Platts, Land and People in Medieval Lincolnshire, *(1985) pp.162 - 163.*

Cures for the Ague

Ague was once common, attracting a range of often extraordinary cures for what was essentially a periodic fever accompanied by shivering.

This disorder used to be very common in Lincolnshire before the drainage and enclosure of the Fens and a great variety of charms were tried.

An old lady who was troubled by this complaint devised the following cure which she insisted worked. At the foot of her bed she nailed three old horseshoes with a hammer placed crosswise upon them. 'When the old 'un comes to shake me, yon'll fix him safe as t'church steeple; he wearn't never pass yon.' She explained: 'It's a chawm. Oi taks the mell I' moy left hand and I taps they shoes an' says

'Feyther, Son and Holy Ghoast,
Naale the divil to this poast.
Throice I strikes with Holy crook,
Won fur God, an' won fur Wod, and won fur Lok.'

It is a strange incantation invoking the pagan gods Woden (the bringer of gifts), Thor with his hammer and Lok, the spirit of evil, who are joined by the Holy Trinity and the Holy Crook.

Henry Winn records another cure which used cabalistic words and signs written on paper which was folded and worn by the sufferer suspended from his neck. The patient was not to know what was written on the paper or the ague would not be cured. Winn says that he knew personally those who said they had been cured by these means and he commented, ' So much for the effect of the imagination!'

He gives the following as an example of one of these charms:

ABACADABRA
BACADABAR
ACADABA
CADAB
ADA
D

Sufferers could also try digging up seven worms from a churchyard, cutting them up small and swallowing them. If all else fails, chips from a gibbet or gallows placed in a bag and worn around the neck will no doubt do the trick.

John Ketteringham, A Lincolnshire Hotchpotch, (1989), p. 25.

The Pox and Typhoid

Plague had disappeared, but the year 1719 was marked by a great mortality, both in this country and elsewhere. The 'epidemic distemper', as Maurice Johnson termed it, may have been typhoid fever as the register at Bolingbroke informs us, 'This was a remarkable dry year, such as had not happened in the memory of man. The hay harvest was the smallest that was ever known.' During the year there were 175 burials at Old Leake, 158 at Sibsey, 117 at Gosberton, 40 at Grimoldby and 34 at Spilsby.

Small pox was rife during the whole of the century. William Stukeley caught the disease in 1706, much to his joy and satisfaction, as he considered at a fitting preliminary for one entering the medical profession. The deaths of his younger brother and family manservant from the same disease would moderate his pleasure. Holbeach suffered from the small pox in 1789 and 1803; in the latter year 'a violent and putrid fever raged' in neighbouring parishes, there being 76 burials at Whaplode. In 1724 Mrs Wesley wrote from Wroot to 'Dear Jacky' that the small pox had been very bad at Epworth most of the summer. 'Our family have all had it except me.' In 1806 in the parish of Stamford St Mary's, there was only one child who had not had the small pox. Inoculation became general about the end of the century.

Medical knowledge had not advanced greatly since 1636 when the physician at Brocklesby postponed giving physic to the Pelham children until the sun should enter the equinoctial. When Sir Pury Cust was ordered to take three pills every night, which were to be followed by two quarts of Epsom Salts every morning, he probably wished for a longer postponement. Quacks abounded: John Wesley found one at Cleethorpes pouring medicine into a man for 'wind in the nerves'. Many of the remedies prescribed for the prevalent ague were loathsome and superstitious, and bleeding was resorted to generally for all kinds of fevers and agues.

At Bardney the schoolmaster bled the boys, and 'Dutch' medicine, Daffy's Elixir, and Sandy's Ague medicine were provided for the poor in the same place. All these contained opium, and in many parts of the county the people were addicted to laudenam before the drainage of the Fens. (About 1775 the Peruvian bark was being used to combat ague by richer people). Tea drinking, which became general towards the end of the century, did much to stop the taking of opium: green tea, which cost 14s. a pound in Skegness and Wainfleet in 1718, was sold in 1783 at 2s. a pound. The increasing consumption of port-wine by the upper classes pre-disposed them to attacks of gout. The Berties regarded the gout as hereditary in their family as the staff. Sir Joseph

Banks, who suffered agonies from the disease, wrote to Thomas Coltman of Hagnaby in 1796: 'I am, thank God, now able to put on my shoes and walk. I have received more benefit than I can describe by the flannel waistcoat which you made me put under my shirt.' Unfortunately, the relief was not permanent, as Sir Joseph towards the close of his life, at times lost the use of his limbs.

Charles Brears, Lincolnshire in the Seventeenth and Eighteenth Centuries *pp. 99-101.*

The Plague Stone

An inconspicuous little byway starts from near Alford station and runs parallel with the line about a mile northwards to Tothby, where it bends round and loses itself in a network of lanes near south Thoresby. At Tothby, under a weeping ash tree on the lawn in front of the old Manor House farm, is an interesting relic of bygone days. It is a stone about a yard square and half a yard thick, once shaped at the corners and with a socket in it. Evidently it is the base of an old churchyard, wayside or market cross of pre-reformation times. And it has been put to use later as a plague-stone, having been for that purpose placed on its edge and half buried probably, and a hole seven inches by five, and two and a half inches deep, cut in the upper side. This was to hold vinegar into which the townspeople put money they gave for the farm produce bought from the country in times of plague.

The great desire was to avoid contact with possibly plague-stricken people. So the country folk brought their poultry, eggs, etc, laid them out at fixed prices near the stone and then retired. Then the town caterer came and took what was wanted, placing the money in the vinegar, and on his retiring in turn, the vendors came and took their money, which was disinfected by its vinegar bath.

W.F. Rawnsley, Highways and Byways of Lincolnshire, *(1914), p. 290.*

Prevalence of diseases 1831

The wife of Wainfleet All Saints rector, the Revd Robert Cholmeley, writing to relatives in 1831, remarked on the prevalence of scarlet fever and whooping cough, one poor woman having lost five of her six children [from the diseases]. People seemed quite ignorant of the dangers of infection [she wrote] and she had known a family ride home in the conveyance that had carried the corpse for burial, and when neighbours showed reluctance to visit children struck down with contagious diseases, the mother would say, 'What harm can my poor bairns do anybody?'

Letters and papers of the Cholmeleys of Wainfleet, 1813-1853. *Lincoln Record Society, vol.59, (1964), pp.38 and 44.*
Winston Kime, Wainfleet Heritage, *(1998), p. 3.*

A Healthy Place

In his paper, *Traces of the Viking Folklore in the Marshland* (1902), the Reverend Robert Marshall Heanley described the Lincolnshire Marshland as 'that great expanse of rich land, of varying width, between the Wolds and the sea, which in spite of its name is about the driest and healthiest district in all England.'

Winston Kime, Wainfleet Heritage, *(1998), p. 3.*

Some Lincolnshire Remedies

Boils. Dissolve some glycerine in a cup standing in a pan of hot water. Then stir in sufficient Epsom Salts to form a paste and spread on the boil.

Chilblains. Put a heaped tablespoon of cattle Epsom Salts and a piece of common soda about the size of a small nut into half a gallon of warm water and soak chilblains for 10 to 15 minutes.

Cramp. Carrying a lucky bone in your shoe will keep off the cramp or wearing a ring made from the hinge of a coffin.

Gout. Take two ounces of soap a day for three months with powdered oyster shell and egg.

Headache. A halter by which anyone has been hanged if tied about the head will cure a headache. Moss, growing upon a human skull if dried, powdered and taken as snuff will also cure a headache.

Nightmare. Nightmares can be prevented if stockings are hung crossways at the foot of the bed. If you lie on your side this will ward off nightmares but if you lie on your back this will probably cause them. Another preventative is to hang a stone with a hole in it at the head of the bed.

Rheumatism. Sufferers from rheumatism can be cured of this common complaint by getting confirmed again. However, if the clergy disapprove of this remedy the patient could try the following recipe: Boil 1oz. of celery seed in a pint of water until reduced to half a pint. Strain and bottle, corking well. Take one teaspoon twice a day for a fortnight. Repeat if necessary.

Rupture. A weak or ruptured child should be drawn through a tree that has been split. The tree is then bound together again and, as the tree unites, the child will gather strength.

Sore throat. If a child has got a sore throat the following remedy should be tried: Take a live frog and put it in the child's mouth. Holding it by the leg let the child suck it to death and the sore throat will disappear.

Swellings. If the hand of a criminal who has been executed be passed nine times over a swelling, it will be dispelled.

John Ketteringham, A Lincolnshire Hotchpotch, *(1989), pp. 46 and 59.*

Moulds in Traditional Lincolnshire Medicine

Soon after the appearance of penicillin, medical historians began a search of the early literature to see if records of the use of this antibiotic could be found which predated Alexander Fleming's original 'official' discovery in 1928. These soon showed that moulds similar to those from which from which we obtain penicillin had been widely used as curatives in folk medicines in Ancient Greece, Ancient China, and in Lincolnshire from the sixteenth to the early twentieth century.

A Greek king of the sixteenth century BC, for example, described how a peasant woman used mould scraped from mouldy cheese to treat his wounded soldiers. The Chinese, 3,000 years ago, used mouldy soya beans to treat infected cuts, wounds and burns. Closer to home, the Boston diarist, Thomas Goodson, noted in 1657that 'white witches', 'wise women' and 'cunning men' around Boston used a mush of mouldy bread in water to treat impetigo, cuts, wounds, burns and all manner of skin infections.

A letter to *The News Chronicle* in 1892 described how 'In many Kesteven farm houses and cottages the Good Friday bun was allowed to hang suspended from the grimy beams of the kitchen ceiling and there were a number of superstitions attached to it. Foremost among these was the tradition that the mouldy portions, removed from it time to time and mushed with water, were suitable as curative agents for many complaints or disorders and these pseudo remedies were exploited to treat both human and cattle'.

A similar practice was evidently widespread elsewhere in Europe, witness this account by Dr E.A. Cliffe. 'It was during my visit through central Europe in 1908 that I came across the fact that almost every farmhouse followed the practice of keeping a mouldy loaf on one of the beams in the kitchen. I was told that this was an old custom and that when any member of the family received an injury such as a cut or bruise, a thin slice of mouldy bread was cut off the loaf, mixed into a paste with water and applied to the wound with a bandage. It was assumed that no infection could result from such a cut.'

Less frequently, mention is also made of the curative virtues of the moulds developed on fruit. Here is an account by Mr D.C. McCarthy of Mablethorpe.

'Many years ago an old aunt of mine (who was 82 and lived in Alford), who appeared to be quite learned in 'cures', read one day in a newspaper of Professor Fleming's discovery of penicillin which was described as resulting from research on the mould. My aunt said in her own inimitable way, 'I had that one before he did.' I know that one of her cures was to collect ten to twelve oranges and place them somewhere where they could get mouldy as soon as possible. She would then carefully remove the greenish mould and make it into some kind of concoction/infusion and use it on abscesses, boils, whitlows and other forms of pustule. She would also administer it orally for a great variety of complaints, and all apparently with complete success.'

Sometimes reference is made to the therapeutic uses of moulds developed on animal products such as lard. For example, this account from Mrs Ida Collingwood: 'My grandfather, when I was young and used to stay with him at Bourne (about the early 1920s), and if we had nasty, sore knees, and cuts and scabs from falling down, used to get his penknife and scrape the ham or bacon side hung from the ceiling (to be cured), salted and green, and put the mouldy fat on a piece of clean linen and grandma used to wrap our knees up and it always cleared and healed our wounds.'

In a similar vein, the following appeared in *The Daily Express* in 1943: 'Mrs Eva Ward of Market Rasen is a little scornful of the new wonder drug that has been discovered from mould called penicillin. Her great-grandmother used to collect all the new copper pennies she could, and old copper kettles, smear them with lard and leave them in a damp place. When the mould had formed she would scrape it off into little boxes and everyone for miles around used to come to her for the remedies for what ailed them.'

The substances used to grow moulds for use in folk medicine were invariably foodstuffs. These substrates tend to become contaminated almost exclusively by the species of *Penicillium* and *Aspergillus* which wage chemical warfare against competing bacteria by releasing a wide range of bacteriocidal antibiotics including penicillin.

Andrew Allen, The Lincolnshire Poacher, *(Autumn 2002) pp.30 - 31.*

Local Remedies

Ethel H. Rudkin was a great collector of local history and folklore. She spent time talking to local people about old customs, remedies for illness, and stories that have been passed from generation to generation. The following are some of the remedies she discovered.

Nosebleeding. To stop this smell the flower of the Yarrow, called locally 'Nosebleed'.

Cramp. Periwinkle placed under the mattress will prevent cramp of the limbs.

Rheumatism. A mole's foot worn on a watch-chain or carried in the pocket is a good preventative.

Sore breasts. Apply cowdung as a poultice.

Piles, to cure. 'Mazeerie' berries (Daphne Mezereon), take and swallow like pills.

Sore Lips. A leaf of houseleek held between the lips, and bruised so that the 'cream' comes out, will be found of great use. An application of houseleek is good for any sore place.

Chapped hands. Quickly cured by putting the backs of hands in one's own water when warm and gently rubbing the backs of the hands until they are dry.

Quinsies. A poultice of black shag tobacco will relieve these.

Ethel H. Rudkin, Lincolnshire Folklore, (1936), pp. 28-3 .

12 · CHURCH AND CHAPEL

After the Reformation

After the Reformation the plight of the Church in the county was a sad one. The clergy were marrying and were often miserably poor. A return of 1565 of livings vacant, mostly through poverty, gives sixty in the Archdeaconry of Lincoln and thirteen in the Archdeaconry of Stow. Later, Archbishop Laud caused enquiries to be made and found that the vicarage of Hogsthorpe was worth but £10 per annum, Mumby £15, Alford £19, and Calceby and Huttoft £13 6s 8d each. The curate of Stow St Mary's petitioned that although he served four towns, and the parsonage was worth £200 a year, he received only £10. As a result many of the clergy had to add to their income by engaging in unclerical pursuits, some of which disgraced their sacred calling. In 1594, the curate of Wyberton kept an ale-house. A curate of Asgarby followed the same calling and stated that he got more by ale than the altar, and would rather leave the church than the ale-house.

Many churches became neglected and were plundered by unscrupulous persons. Early in the seventeenth century the lead on the church porch at Ruskington was replaced by straw and the church was indecent, being unpaved and not whitened. The Chancel at Wainfleet St Mary, the north aisle of Crowland, and the chancel of Little Steeping were robbed of their lead and thatched. At Grantham the windows were daubed up, the organs taken away, and no copy of the Holy Scriptures [left] in the church. The churchwardens in Partney had daubed up a window and allowed swine to root up the bodies of the dead in the churchyard. Much deliberate destruction was wrought by extremists, who thought that the work started at the Reformation should be completed. One of the Boston churchwardens, Atherton Hough, climbed the steeple and broke off the arm and hand of the figure of St Botolph, under the impression it was an image of the pope. The soldiers, pressed for the hated expedition against the Scots in 1640, were doubtless guilty of much destruction when stationed at Sleaford and in the neighbourhood of Gainsborough. Tradition, like the lying jade she usually is, has blamed Cromwell for their misdeeds.

At a time when religious feeling ran very high, there was often brawling within the sacred building. At Edlington, one of the parishioners, who was probably a Roman Catholic, was guilty of 'irreverently with scorn fleering [mocking] and laughing in church'. The Puritan minister at Gosberton reviled his neighbours in the church, calling them brazen-faces and liars. In Skirbeck in 1621, Mr Strangridge irreverently snatched the hour glass from the pulpit immediately before the sermon 'and did so delaye it about halfe a quarter of an hour'.

Charles Brears, Lincolnshire in the Seventeenth and Eighteenth Centuries, *(1940), pp. 22-23*

Gilbert of Sempringham and the Gilbertine Order.

Gilbert was born about 1085 at Sempringham near Billingborough and was the son of Jocelin, a Norman knight, who came from Normandy with William the Conqueror. His mother was a Saxon 'of inferior origin' and was said to have dreamed before Gilbert's birth that she was holding a round moon in her lap, which was taken to be a sign that the child would rise to greatness.

Because of a deformity, Gilbert was unable to follow the knightly pursuits of his father. It was believed he was shunned because of his repulsive appearance. He went to France, probably to the monastery of Citeaux, and on his return to England in 1123 his father gave him the livings of Sempringham and Torrington.

Gilbert gave the revenue of these benefices to the poor and founded and taught in free schools in his parishes. He lived in a room over the porch in the church at Sempringham and he decided to found a convent to which women could retire from the world in order to devote themselves to study and worship. The Priory of Sempringham was founded in 1135 and the new Order of Gilbertines was approved by the Pope, the King and Bishop Alexander of Lincoln. Gilbertine Priories were founded at Alvingham, North Ormsby, Six Hills, West Torrington and Lincoln. Others followed until there was a total of thirteen houses for women. Men were introduced into a house to help with the heavy work but were kept strictly separate from the nuns. Although Gilbert was renowned for his gentleness, he made strict rules for discipline.

Gilbert was particularly interested in education and taught by example. He set a high example, not only by his own learning and piety but also by his humility and energy. Numerous miracles were ascribed to him. In London, fire consumed the houses surrounding the one in which he was staying but he remained praying and the fire consumed all but the room in which he was situated.

In 1165 Gilbert and his Priors were summoned to Westminster, charged with assisting Thomas à Becket. Gilbert said he would suffer exile rather than say he was innocent of the charge because he believed he was right to assist the Archbishop as head of his Church. The charge was dismissed by Henry II. After his death at the supposed age of 106, the order continued to grow and at the Dissolution there were twenty-six Gilbertine houses in England.

Gilbert was canonised in 1202 and his tomb in the Priory Church at Sempringham became a place of pilgrimage. St Gilbert's feast day is 4 February.

John Ketteringham, Lincolnshire People, (1995), p. 42.

St Guthlac

Another saint connected with the county is St Guthlac who lived in a tiny cell at Croyland (Crowland) Abbey, was ordained, and after his death his body was embalmed and revered as that of a saint.

Now St Guthlac is no legendary saint; he was a member of the Mercian royal house, who, tired of soldiering, sought a retirement from the world; and certainly few better places could be found than what was then a desolate, reedy waste of waters at the point where Cambridgeshire, Northamptonshire and Lincolnshire meet by the edge of Deeping Fen. No road led to it and the Fenmen's boats were the only means of passage.

Guthlac was, we are told. The son of Penwald, a Mercian nobleman, and he was very likely born not far from Croyland. After nine years' military service he entered the monastery of Hrypadon, or Repton, and after two years' study resolved to take up the life of an Anchorite. So, in defiance of the evil spirits who were reputed to have their abode there, and who were probably nothing but the shrieking sea-gulls and the melancholy cries of the bittern and curlew, he landed on a bit of dry ground two miles to the north-east of Croyland, now called Anchor-Church-Hill, just east of the Spalding road. Here were some British or Saxon burial mounds, on one of which he set up his hut and chapel, while his sister Pega established herself a few miles to the south-west, at Peakirk. He landed on his island on St Bartholomew's day, August 24, 699, a young man of twenty-six, and here he was visited by Bishop Haedda, who ordained him in 705. In 709, Aethelbald being outlawed by his cousin King Coelred, took sanctuary with St Guthlac, who prophesied to him that he would one day be king, and without bloodshed. St Guthlac died in 713 or 714, but Aethelbald, who had vowed to build a monastery for Guthlac if he ever could, did become king in 716, and in gratitude built the first stone church and endowed a monastery for Benedictines at Croyland. Naturally St Guthlac was the patron saint and to him was joined St Bartholomew, on whose day he had first come to Croyland.

W.F. *Rawnsley,* Highways and Byways of Lincolnshire, *(1914), pp. 483 – 485.*

Crowland Abbey

The interior contains some very curious inscriptions and memorials, particularly one tablet in commemoration of William of Wermington, who was in charge of the repairs to the west tower in 1427. The inscription in Norman French should be of special interest to Freemasons, proving as it does, the undeniable existence of Freemasonry in the fifteenth century... Which, being interpreted, is:

'Here lies Master William of Wermington, the Mason, on the soul of whom, God, of His Grace give absolution.'

The Master Mason is represented as wearing a monk's cowl and habit, while he carries in his hand a pair of compasses and a square. He is sometimes called William of Croyland, and was master of the works when the vaulting was erected in the roof of the present church. The stone carries the mark of the lodge, a cross with four nail ends; the same mark may be seen on the west front of the abbey. The memorial is a complete sermon in stone. 'Live within your means (compasses) and upon the square.'

Christopher Marlowe, The Fen Country, *(1925), pp. 45- 46*

A Linguistic Vicar: Henry Hodgson, LL.D.

Henry Hodgson (1753- 1815) was a farmer's son, born in Toft-by-Newton near Market Rasen. He graduated from Peterhouse, Cambridge and went on to study medicine in Edinburgh before taking holy orders and becoming vicar of Tealby and Corringham. A memorial on the wall of Tealby church commemorates his life.

Hodgson has been described as 'a typical specimen of a Liberal churchman.' He was the author of many pamphlets on the American and French revolutions and a very frequent contributor to *The Gentleman's Magazine,* as well as writer of many letters and sermons. He was in Tealby when a ploughman turned up the Tealby Hoard of Henry II silver pennies in November 1807, though his writings about this seem not to have survived. Almost certainly the landowner, George Tennyson, would have consulted Dr Hodgson about the find.

The Reverend Dr Hodgson was a fairly large landowner in Tealby owning various parcels of land amounting to some sixty acres, much of this in the Tealby Thorpe area. One of his fields was called Hang Dog Close. The land would have come to him as tythe as he would have inherited very little from his parents at Toft.

Research reveals very little about Henry Hodgson's wife, although he had a son, Augustus, born (probably in Tealby) in 1802.

Henry Hodgson appears to have been a man of some character, unafraid to tread on parish and diocesan toes. From 20 July 1806 to 29 March 1807 he closed the church . . .

' . . . on account of thorough repairs and pewing. The reading desk and pulpit before the former of those days were on the south of the first pillar from the chancel on the south side of the middle alley [sic]. The body of the church old and much decayed or decaying seats,' he wrote.

On 15 October 1814 he received a circular letter from Dr Prettyman, the Archdeacon of Lincoln, asking parish priests to send in returns of National Schools in their areas. Hodgson's sharp reply cannot have endeared him to his Episcopal superiors –

'I, Henry Hodgson, vicar of the said parish (of Tealby alias Tevilby) do profess my ignorance of the meaning of the expression 'National School' . . . if he is favoured with an explanation of what is meant by 'National School' he will give, if necessary, a more explicit answer...'

He went on to describe Tealby.

' . . . the parish is large –120 or 130 inhabited houses. There are in it two or three schools – one of the inferior class . . . the Writing School is supported by subscription of the parish . . .

Jim Murray, Tealby Gleanings, *(1995) p.80*

A Most Remarkable Family

John and Charles Wesley, the best known of this large family, were two of the children of Samuel Wesley, the rector of Epworth. The author of this extract omits to mention the Christian name of Mrs Wesley, even though he describes her as 'a remarkable woman.'

John, the fifteenth child, was the middle brother of three, who all had a first-rate public school and university education, getting scholarships both at school and college: John at Charterhouse, the others under Dr Busby at Westminster, and all at Christchurch, Oxford, whence John, at the age of seventeen, wrote to his mother, 'I propose to be busy as long as I live'. Eventually he became a Fellow of Lincoln. The whole family were as clever as could be, and the seven daughters had a first-rate education from their father and mother at home. Mrs Wesley was a remarkable woman, a Jacobite – which was somewhat disconcerting to her husband, who had written in defence of the Revolution – and a person of strong independence of spirit. Of her daughters, Hetty was the cleverest; and she is the only one who gives no account of the famous 'Epworth ghost', which is significant, when both her parents and all her sisters wrote a full account of it. Hetty's poems are of a very high standard of excellence, and it is more than likely that she wrote the verse part – for it is partly in prose dialogue – of 'Eupolis' Hymn to the Creator', which is far better than anything else attributed to Sam Wesley. He died in 1735, and John, who had been curate to him at Epworth and Wroot (the livings went together), left the neighbourhood; and the place that had been home to one of Lincolnshire's most remarkable families for nearly forty years knew them no more.

Lincoln, however, saw John Wesley, for he preached in the castle yard in 1780, as his father had done seventy-five years earlier, when he was spitefully imprisoned for debt. He was preaching at Lincoln again in 1788 and again in July 1790 in the new Wesleyan Chapel. Eight months later he died.

John Wesley had been denied access to the Church of England pulpits for fifty years, 1738 – 1788. Even when he preached at Epworth in 1742, it was from his father's tombstone; and in most cases his congregations, which were often very large, were gathered together in the open air. We hear of him preaching to a large assemblage in the rain at north Elkington, on April 6, 1759; and also at Scawby, Tealby, Louth, Brigg and Cleethorpes; but in June 1788, he notes in his diary: 'Preached at Grimsby, the vicar reading prayers (a notable change this), not so crowded in the memory of man'. Each member of the Wesleyan Conference sits in Wesley's chair on his inauguration, and has Wesley's Bible handed to him to hold, as John Wesley himself holds it in his left hand in the statue.

W.F. *Rawnsley*, Highways and Byways in Lincolnshire, *(1914), pp. 210-212.*

A Prolific Writer of Hymns

Charles Wesley was a great supporter both of Methodism and of his brother John. He was also a prolific writer of hymns, writing over 5000, many of which are regularly sung today – including 'Christ, whose glory fills the skies', 'Gentle Jesus, meek and mild', and 'Love divine, all loves excelling'. One of his most stirring must surely be the following:

> Soldiers of Christ, arise
> And put your armour on;
> Strong in the strength which God supplies,
> Through his eternal Son;
>
> Strong in the Lord of Hosts,
> And in his mighty power;
> Who in the strength of Jesus trusts
> Is more than conqueror.
>
> Stand then in His great might,
> With all his strength endued;
> And take, to arm you for the fight,
> The panoply of God.
>
> To keep your armour bright
> Attend with constant care,
> Still walking in your Captain's sight,
> And watching unto prayer.
>
> From strength to strength go on;
> Wrestle, and fight, and pray;
> Tread all the powers of darkness down,
> And win the well-fought day;
>
> That having all things done,
> And all your conflicts past,
> Ye may o'ercome, through Christ alone,
> And stand entire at last.

Halton Holgate

Halton Holgate stands on the very edge of the Wold, where the green-sand terminates, and looks far across the Fen to Boston. The name of the village is always properly pronounced by the natives, Halton Hollygate, i.e., hollow gate or way; for the descending road has been cut through the green-sand rock, and where the cutting is deepest a pretty timber footbridge is thrown over it, leading from the rectory to the churchyard. The garden lawn has, or had, two fine old mulberry trees. These were once more common – for in the reign of James I an order went out for planting mulberry trees in all rectory gardens with a view to the encouragement of the silk trade by the breeding and feeding of silkworms, whose favourite diet is the mulberry leaf. From the garden, 'Boston stump' is visible eighteen miles to the south. The church is a particularly handsome one with massive well-proportioned tower, and large belfry windows, eight three-light clerestory windows on either side and a fine south porch of Ancaster stone. The rest is built of the beautifully tinted local green-sand, with quoins of harder Clipsham stone. Inside it is spacious, with lofty octagonal pillars; it is seated throughout with oak, and has several good old oak poppy-heads and some large, modern ones copied from Winthorpe and carved by a Halton carpenter. Here it is worth notice that for the last hundred years Halton has never been without wood-workers of unusual talent.

W.F. Rawnsley, Highways & Byways of Lincolnshire (1914), p. 329-330.

13 · EPITAPHS

Lincolnshire's churchyards are a source of endless fascination, not just for their often glorious setting, but because of their tombstones. We can learn much about someone from the inscription on their tombstone. Some are angry, some sorrowful, and others simply funny. They all seem to encapsulate the essence of the person commemorated. Here is a selection of epitaphs discovered on gravestones and brass tablets.

The Reverend G E Jeans wrote the following about one of the sepulchral brasses of Lincolnshire in 1911.

In the tiny church of Lusby, close to the battlefield of Winceby, there is a small brass plate on a slab which bears, as far as I can make out, the date 1555. It has a pretty little inscription in verse as a dialogue between a wife and a husband. It runs:

'My flesh in hope doth rest and slepe
　　In earth here to remayne.
My spirit to Christ I gyve to kepe
　　Till I do rise again.'

'And I wyth you in hope agre,
　　Though I yet here abyde,
In full purpose if Goddes will be
　　To ly down by your syde.'

*The tombstone of Daniel Lambert, made in Leicester of Swithland
slate, is still a place of pilgrimage in St Martin's churchyard, Stamford.*

In Remembrance of
that PRODIGY in NATURE
DANIEL LAMBERT
a Native of LEICESTER
who was possessed of
an exalted and convivial Mind
and, in personal Greatness
had no COMPETITOR:
He measured three Feet one Inch round the LEG
nine Feet four Inches round the body
and weighed
FIFTY TWO STONE ELEVEN POUNDS
He departed this life
on the 21st June
1809
AGED 39 YEARS
As a Testimony of Respect
this Stone is erected
by his Friends
in Leicester.
                                        Stamford

*William Pepper, who died in 1783, has his life remembered concisely
in St John's Church, Stamford. The stone is very worn but you can just
make out the words.*

Though hot by name, yet mild by nature
I bore goodwill to every creature
I brewed fine ale and sold it too
And unto each I gave his due.
                                        Stamford

The death of Samuel Stockton did not come naturally:

This stone is erected in memory of Mr Samuel Stockton late of Ashley in the parish of Leigh and County of Lancaster who was most barbarously murdered near this place on the eighth of December 1768 for which murder one Philip Hooton was tried and condemned at Lincoln Assize and afterwards executed and hung in chains in the very place where the horrid deed was committed.

Surfleet

The place where William Smith, a popular huntsman, was killed falling from his horse, is remembered in the following manner:

This stone the name of William Smith records,
The Huntsman, skilled, of two of Yarbro's Lords –
Honest and true, of temper well approved,
By Master honoured, and by field beloved;
No need to paint that well-known form and face,
Which stampt on memory, find a welcome place
In the warm hearts that knew him – they recall,
By covet side, in cottage, farm and Hall
(Where friend meets friend beside the yule-log's glow,
And kindly feelings swell and overflow),
Those happy days, when on the breeze were borne
'Will's' tuneful holloa and his echoing horn,
Cheering his gallant pack, so stout and bold,
A perfect horseman, as e're crossed the Wold!
And as the vision fades, too bright to last,
They sigh to think those days are now the past.
No need of aught, for such as knew him best,
To keep in mind their valued friend at rest –
But for posterity, this stone shall tell
The fatal spot where, midst his friends, he fell
And bid them ponder, both in faith and fear,
Hope frail the tenure of man's sojourn here.

Laceby

A loving daughter praises her mother:

Sacred to the Memory of
Anna Maria Amcotts
wife of Sir Wharton Amcotts of Kettlethorpe
in this county, Bart., daughter of
Vincent and Elizabeth Amcotts of Harrington
born 11th of April 1725, died 1st of July, 1800
In her were united the mild virtues of a Christian
with every female excellence
As she lived beloved she died lamented
more particularly
by her daughter Elizabeth Ingilby Amcotts
wife of Sir John Ingliby of Ripley
in the county of York, Bart.
who out of grateful respect to her memory on her death
took the name of Amcotts
and hath erected this monument to perpetuate
the remembrance of her beloved parent
                              Kettlethorpe

In Lutton church there is a black stone inscribed with the following:

> Thy busy and inquisitive eye
> seems to demand that here
> doth lie
> If I must disclose my trust
> T'is great lemented [sic] prudent Dust
> If yet unsatisfyed thou'lt know
> And eurg [sic] me further Read below
> Here lyeth the body of Mr Ruben Parke of Lutton who
> deceased the
> 10 of July, 1659, in the 63d yeare
> of his age.
> Hence Quarrell Nature tell she shall
> Repeate his climactericall.
>   Lutton

In a lighter vein a headstone in Corby [Glen] acknowledges the virtues of Joseph Wright who was 60 years old when he died in 1835.

Beneath this stone facetious wight
Lies all that's left of poor Joe Wright

Few hearts with greater kindness warmed
Few heads with knowledge more informed
With pleasant wit and humour broad
He please the Peasant, Squire or Lord
At length old Death with visage queer
Assumed Joe's trade of auctioneer
Made him the lot to practice on
With going, going and anon
He knocked him down, so poor Joe's gone.

Some memorials are confusing. Take this one from the church in Corringham, for instance.

Anno Dni. mdcxxxi
To the glory of God and for the pious remem
brance of their dear Brethren Robert and Thomas
Broxholme, Gent., late of Corringham in the countie of
Lincoln deceased and here interred Henry and Mary
Broxholme (yet surviving) have erected this memorial
who with their deceased brethren afore names having
lived together about 60 years and for the most part of
this time in one family and most brotherly concord
comfortable to each other beloved of their neighbours charitable to
the poor
constant in the profession of the true
Religion doe suppose (by the favour of God) to dye
In the same faith and here to rest together with them in
One and the same Hope of a glorious Resurrection
Though to be foure in Person they were knowne
Yet both in will and mind they were but one
One Father and one Mother them begot
And they made up one four-fold true love knot
They kept one Family and which is rare

They had no jarring neither discords there
None of them were agreaved or discontent
What either or the other gave or spent
In one plain path they waited all their daies
Not judging nor invieing others waies
No so much seeking for the world's esteeme
As to be truly that which they did seem.
One Faith one Hope one Love they living had
Which them the members of one Body made
Though none of them had husband child or wife
They mist no blessing of the married life
For to the Poor they ever were indeed
Of Husband Wife and Parent to their need
Thus they who knew them witness and beleeve
That when immortal Bodys they receeve
They shall make up the Vergine traine of those
Who wait upon the LAMB where'er he goes.

In Somerby church there is a monument to Jane Brownlow, daughter of Sir Richard Brownlow of Humby, which is unusual because it describes her physical appearance rather than her spiritual attributes.

She was of a solid, serious temper, of a competent
Stature and a fayre compleaciton, whoes soul
Now is perfectly butyfyed with the friution of
God in glory and whose body in her dew time
He will raise to the enjoyment of the same.

Sir Adrian Scrope is remembered with the following words:

Tombs are but dumb day-books, they will not keepe
There names alive who in these wombs doe sleepe,
But who would pen the virtues of this knight
A story not an epitaph must write.

                                    South Cockerington

In the north aisle of Addlethorpe church there is a simple epitaph to Thomas Ely.

> Plain in his form but rich he was in mind
> Religious, quiet, honest, meek and kind.

At Croft in the sixteenth century, George Bonde, a 'Docter of Divinitie, wrote a Latin inscription for his own epitaph which, translated becomes:

> I was Bond a physician, now I am food for worms,
> The earth covers my body, my spirit seeks the stars,
> From difficult studies, anxiety, diseases and old age
> Life was a burden; death is a welcome rest for me.

About four miles from Friskney is Wrangle, the name meaning a lake or mere of reeds. In the chancel of the church there is a memorial, dated 1503, to John Reed 'sum time Marchant of Calys and Margaret his wyfe':

> This for man, when ye wind blows
> Make the mill grind,
> But ever on thyn oune soul
> Have thou in mind,
> That thou givys with thy hand
> Yt thou shalt find,
> And yt thou levys thy executor
> Comys far behynde.
> Do thou for thy selfe while ye have space.
> To pray Jesu for mercy and grace,
> In heaven to have a place.

Finally, in Crowland Abbey there is a stone that marks the grave of Abraham Baly who died in 1704:

Beneath this place six foot in length against Ye Clark's pew lyeth the body of Mr Baly and the bodies of Mary his widow, of Abraham his son and of two otheres who died in infancy.

Above the stone were the following words:

Man's life is like
Unto a Winter's Day
Some brake their fast
and so depart away
Others stay dinner, then
    depart full fed,
    The oldest age butt
    supps and goes to bed
    O Reader then behold and see
    as wee are now, so must you bee
        1705

ACKNOWLEDGEMENTS

I am indebted to the staff at Stamford Library, particularly Jackie Pitcher (senior library assistant), Lyn Beechby, Linda Oliver, Denise De Salis, Ann Turner and Beryl Wallace who are always so helpful; to the staff at Stamford Museum and at Lincoln Library; to Judy Theobald, editor of *Lincolnshire Life*, for reading the typescript and to Anthony and Pat Bradley for the bolthole in Lyme Regis where I completed the final draft.

I am grateful to the following for allowing the inclusion of both prose and poetry which remains in copyright: B.T. Batsford for M.W. Barley's *Lincolnshire & The Fens*; A. Brown & Sons for Charles Brears' *Lincolnshire in the 17th and 18th centuries* and J.E. Swaby's *The Marshmen*; Robert Hale for John Bygott's *Lincolnshire*, Michael Lloyd's *Portrait of Lincolnshire* and Edward Storey's *Spirit of the Fens*; Leicester Museums & Art Gallery for David Clarke's *Daniel Lambert* (1973 third edition); Roy Fisk for *Lincolnshire Medley*; Bryan Forbes' *A Divided Life*, reproduced with permission of Curtis Brown Group Ltd, London on behalf of Bryan Forbes Copyright ©; Arrival Press for Suzy Goodall's *Eastern England Poets*; Countryside Books for Adrian Gray's *Tales of Old Lincolnshire*, Patrick Otter's *Lincolnshire Airfields in the Second World War* and Polly Howat's *Ghosts and Legends of Lincolnshire and the Fen Country*; John Ketteringham M.B.E for extracts from his *Lincolnshire People* (3rd book in series *Lincolnshire Natives and Others* just published) and *A Lincolnshire Hotchpotch* (the first in a series of 3); The King's England Press for Arthur Mee's *The King's England, Lincolnshire*; Alan Sutton Publishing for Graham Platts' *Land and People in Medieval Lincolnshire*; Books by Baron for David Robinson's *The Book of the Lincolnshire Seaside* and David Kaye's *The Book of Grimsby*, both published by Barracuda Books; Oakwood Press for Stewart Squires' *The Lincolnshire Potato Railways*; Pearson

Educational for David Steel's *A Lincolnshire Village*; for the extract from *Lincolnshire* by Henry Thorold, published by Pimlico, reprinted by permission of The Random House Group Ltd; Penguin Group (UK) for Danny Danziger's *The Cathedral* and David Higham Associates and Penguin Group (UK) for Wing Commander Guy Gibson's *Enemy Coast Ahead*; The University of Hull Press for B.J. Davey's *Rural Crime in the Eighteenth Century*; Oxford University Press for Edward Gillett's *A History of Grimsby*; David Morton of Firs Publishing for Winston Kime's *Wainfleet Heritage*; Michael Bloch for James Lees-Milne's *Ancestral Voices*; Faber & Faber for Jack Yates' and Henry Thorold's *Lincolnshire, A Shell Guide*; *Lincolnshire Life* magazine for the extract from an article by Tom Herbert.

The publishers have endeavoured to contact all holders of copyright, but will be pleased to correct any omissions or errors in future editions.